DEMOCRACY
MATTERS

DEMOCRACY MATTERS

*Winning the Fight
Against Imperialism*

Cornel West

THE PENGUIN PRESS

New York

2004

THE PENGUIN PRESS
Published by the Penguin Group
Penguin Group (USA) Inc., 375 Hudson Street, New York, New York 10014, U.S.A. ·
Penguin Group (Canada), 10 Alcorn Avenue, Toronto, Ontario, Canada M4V 3B2 (a division
of Pearson Penguin Canada Inc.) · Penguin Books Ltd, 80 Strand, London WC2R 0RL,
England · Penguin Ireland, 25 St. Stephen's Green, Dublin 2, Ireland (a division of
Penguin Books Ltd) · Penguin Books Australia Ltd, 250 Camberwell Road, Camberwell,
Victoria 3124, Australia (a division of Pearson Australia Group Pty Ltd) · Penguin Books
India Pvt Ltd, 11 Community Centre, Panchsheel Park, New Delhi–110 017, India · Penguin
Group (NZ), Cnr Airborne and Rosedale Roads, Albany, Auckland, New Zealand (a division
of Pearson New Zealand Ltd) · Penguin Books (South Africa) (Pty) Ltd, 24 Sturdee Avenue,
Rosebank, Johannesburg 2196, South Africa

Penguin Books Ltd, Registered Offices:
80 Strand, London WC2R 0RL, England

First published in 2004 by The Penguin Press,
a member of Penguin Group (USA) Inc.

Page 220 constitutes an extension of this copyright page.

The composition "Where Ya At?" with lyrics by DA Smart
and others appears on *One Million Strong: The Album*.

Library of Congress Cataloging-in-Publication Data
West, Cornel.
Democracy matters : winning the fight against imperialism / Cornel West.
p.   cm.
Includes index.
ISBN 1-59420-029-7
1. Democracy. 2. Imperialism. 3. Democracy—United States.
I. Title.
JC423.W384 2004
321.8—dc22   2004050520
This book is printed on acid-free paper. ∞

1   3   5   7   9   10   8   6   4   2

Printed in the United States of America
Designed by Amanda Dewey

To five great democratic teachers

MARTIN KILSON
Pioneering Harvard professor, lifelong mentor,
and towering black intellectual

PRESTON WILLIAMS
Path-blazing Harvard professor, grand exemplar of the legacy
of Martin Luther King Jr., and dear godfather

SHELDON WOLIN
Sterling Princeton professor, blessed thesis adviser,
and the greatest theorist of democracy in our time

STANLEY ARONOWITZ
Grand public intellectual, lifelong comrade,
and fellow lover of deep democracy

DILAN ZEYTUN WEST
Beloved daughter, bearer of elegant style,
and the source of great joy and love

CONTENTS

1

DEMOCRACY MATTERS ARE FRIGHTENING IN OUR TIME

We have frequently printed the word Democracy, yet I cannot too often repeat that it is a word the real gist of which still sleeps, quite unawakened, notwithstanding the resonance and the many angry tempests out of which its syllables have come, from pen or tongue. It is a great word, whose history, I suppose, remains unwritten, because that history has yet to be enacted.

—WALT WHITMAN, *Democratic Vistas* (1871)

To be an Afro-American, or an American black, is to be in the situation, intolerably exaggerated, of all those who have ever found themselves part of a civilization which they could in no wise honorably defend—which they were compelled, indeed, endlessly to attack and condemn—and who yet spoke out of the most passionate love, hoping to make the kingdom new, to make it honorable and worthy of life.

—JAMES BALDWIN, *No Name in the Street* (1972)

A decade ago I wrote *Race Matters* in order to spark a candid public conversation about America's most explosive issue and most difficult dilemma: the ways in which the vicious legacy of white supremacy contributes to the arrested development of

American democracy. This book—the sequel to *Race Matters*—will look unflinchingly at the waning of democratic energies and practices in our present age of the American empire. There is a deeply troubling deterioration of democratic powers in America today. The rise of an ugly imperialism has been aided by an unholy alliance of the plutocratic elites and the Christian Right, and also by a massive disaffection of so many voters who see too little difference between two corrupted parties, with blacks being taken for granted by the Democrats, and with the deep disaffection of youth. The energy of the youth support for the Howard Dean campaign and avid participation in the recent antiglobalization protests are promising signs, however, of the potential to engage them.

As I've traveled across this country giving speeches and attending gatherings for the past thirty years, I've always been impressed by the intelligence, imagination, creativity, and humor of the American people, then found myself wondering how we end up with such mediocre and milquetoast leaders in public office. It's as if the best and brightest citizens boycott elected public office, while the most ambitious go into the private sector. In a capitalist society that is where the wealth, influence, and status are. But we've always been a capitalist society, and we've had some quality leaders in the past. Why the steep decline? As with sitcoms on television, the standards have dropped so low, we cannot separate a joke from an insult. When Bush smiles after his carefully scripted press conferences of little substance, we do not know whether he is laughing at us or getting back at us as we laugh at him—as the press meanwhile hurries to concoct a story out of his clichés and shibboleths.

In our market-driven empire, elite salesmanship to the demos has taken the place of genuine democratic leadership. The majority of voting-age citizens do not vote. They are not stupid (though shortsighted). They know that political leadership is confined to two parties that are both parasitic on corporate money and interests. To choose one or the other is a little like black people choosing between the left-wing and right-wing versions of the Dred Scott decision. There is a difference but not much—though every difference does matter.

Yet a narrow rant against the new imperialism or emerging plutocracy is not enough. Instead we must dip deep into often-untapped wells of our democratic tradition to fight the imperialist strain and plutocratic impulse in American life. We must not allow our elected officials—many beholden to unaccountable corporate elites—to bastardize and pulverize the precious word *democracy* as they fail to respect and act on genuine democratic ideals.

The problems plaguing our democracy are not only ones of disaffection and disillusionment. The greatest threats come in the form of the rise of three dominating, antidemocratic dogmas. These three dogmas, promoted by the most powerful forces in our world, are rendering American democracy vacuous. The first dogma of free-market fundamentalism posits the unregulated and unfettered market as idol and fetish. This glorification of the market has led to a callous corporate-dominated political economy in which business leaders (their wealth and power) are to be worshipped—even despite the recent scandals—and the most powerful corporations are delegated magical powers of salvation rather than relegated to democratic scrutiny concerning both the ethics of their business practices and their treatment of workers. This largely un-examined and unquestioned dogma that supports the policies of both Democrats and Republicans in the United States—and those of most political parties in other parts of the world—is a major threat to the quality of democratic life and the well-being of most peoples across the globe. It yields an obscene level of wealth in-equality, along with its corollary of intensified class hostility and hatred. It also redefines the terms of what we should be striving for in life, glamorizing materialistic gain, narcissistic pleasure, and the pursuit of narrow individualistic preoccupations—especially for young people here and abroad.

Free-market fundamentalism—just as dangerous as the reli-gious fundamentalisms of our day—trivializes the concern for pub-lic interest. The overwhelming power and influence of plutocrats and oligarchs in the economy put fear and insecurity in the hearts of anxiety-ridden workers and render money-driven, poll-obsessed elected officials deferential to corporate goals of profit, often at the cost of the common good. This illicit marriage of cor-porate and political elites—so blatant and flagrant in our time—not only undermines the trust of informed citizens in those who rule over them. It also promotes the pervasive sleepwalking of the pop-ulace, who see that the false prophets are handsomely rewarded with money, status, and access to more power. This profit-driven vision is sucking the democratic life out of American society.

In short, the dangerous dogma of free-market fundamental-ism turns our attention away from schools to prisons, from work-ers' conditions to profit margins, from health clinics to high-tech facial surgeries, from civic associations to pornographic Internet sites, and from children's care to strip clubs. The fundamentalism of the market puts a premium on the activities of buying and selling, consuming and taking, promoting and advertising, and devalues community, compassionate charity, and improvement of the general quality of life. How ironic that in America we've moved so quickly from Martin Luther King Jr.'s "Let Freedom Ring!" to "Bling! Bling!"—as if freedom were reducible to simply having material toys, as dictated by free-market fundamentalism.

2.The second prevailing dogma of our time is aggressive militarism, of which the new policy of preemptive strike against potential enemies is but an extension. This new doctrine of U.S. foreign policy goes far beyond our former doctrine of preventive war. It green-lights political elites to sacrifice U.S. soldiers—who are disproportionately working class and youth of color—in adventurous crusades. This dogma posits military might as salvific in a world in which he who has the most and biggest weapons is the most moral and masculine, hence worthy of policing others. In practice, this dogma takes the form of unilateral intervention, colonial invasion, and armed occupation abroad. It has fueled a foreign policy that shuns multilateral cooperation of nations and undermines international structures of deliberation. Fashioned out of the cowboy mythology of the American frontier fantasy, the dogma of aggressive militarism is a lone-ranger strategy that employs "spare-no-enemies" tactics. It guarantees a perennial resorting to the immoral and base manner of settling conflict, namely, the perpetration of the very sick and cowardly terrorism it claims to contain and eliminate. On the domestic front, this dogma expands police power, augments the prison-industrial complex, and legitimates unchecked male power (and violence) at home and in the workplace. It views crime as a monstrous enemy to crush (targeting poor people) rather than as an ugly behavior to change (by addressing the conditions that often encourage such behavior).

As with the bully on the block, one's own interests and aims define what is moral and one's own anxieties and insecurities dictate what is masculine. Yet the use of naked force to resolve conflict often backfires. The arrogant hubris that usually accompanies this use of force tends to lead toward instability—and even destruction—in the regions where we have sought to impose our will. Violence is readily deployed by those who cloak themselves in innocence—those unwilling to examine themselves and uninterested in counting the number of innocent victims they kill. Note the Bush administration's callous disregard for both the U.S. soldiers and innocent Iraqis killed in our recent adventurous invasion. The barbaric abuse of prisoners at Abu Ghraib is a flagrant example.

(3) The third prevailing dogma in this historic moment is escalating authoritarianism. This dogma is rooted in our understandable paranoia toward potential terrorists, our traditional fear of too many liberties, and our deep distrust of one another. The Patriot Act is but the peak of an iceberg that has widened the scope of the repression of our hard-earned rights and hard-fought liberties. The Supreme Court has helped lead the way with its support of the Patriot Act. There are, however, determined democrats on the Court who are deeply concerned, as expressed in a recent speech of Justice Ruth Bader Ginsburg: "On important issues," she said, "like the balance between liberty and security, if the public doesn't care, then the security side is going to overweigh the other." The

cowardly terrorist attacks of 9/11 have been cannon fodder for the tightening of surveillance. The loosening of legal protection and slow closing of meaningful access to the oversight of governmental activities—measures deemed necessary in the myopic view of many—are justified by the notion that safety trumps liberty and security dictates the perimeters of freedom.

Meanwhile the market-driven media—fueled by our vast ideological polarization and abetted by profit-hungry monopolies—have severely narrowed our political "dialogue." The major problem is not the vociferous shouting from one camp to the other; rather it is that many have given up even being heard. We are losing the very value of dialogue—especially respectful communication—in the name of the sheer force of naked power. This is the classic triumph of authoritarianism over the kind of questioning, compassion, and hope requisite for any democratic experiment.

We have witnessed similar developments in our schools and universities—increasing monitoring of viewpoints, disrespecting of those with whom one disagrees, and foreclosing of the common ground upon which we can listen and learn. The major culprit here is not "political correctness," a term coined by those who tend to trivialize the scars of others and minimize the suffering of victims while highlighting their own wounds. Rather the challenge is mustering the courage to scrutinize *all* forms of dogmatic policing of dialogue and to shatter *all* authoritarian strategies of silencing voices. We must respect the scars and wounds of each one of us—even if we are sometimes wrong (or right!).

Democracy matters are frightening in our time precisely because the three dominant dogmas of free-market fundamentalism, aggressive militarism, and escalating authoritarianism are snuffing out the democratic impulses that are so vital for the deepening and spread of democracy in the world. In short, we are experiencing the sad American imperial devouring of American democracy. This historic devouring in our time constitutes an unprecedented gangsterization of America—an unbridled grasp at power, wealth, and status. And when the most powerful forces in a society—and an empire—promote a suffocation of democratic energies, the very future of genuine democracy is jeopardized.

How ironic that 9/11—a vicious attack on innocent civilians by gangsters—becomes the historic occasion for the full-scale gangsterization of America. Do we now live in a postdemocratic age in which the very "democratic" rhetoric of an imperial America hides the waning of a democratic America? Are there enough democratic energies here and abroad to fight for and win back our democracy given the undeniable power of the three dominant dogmas that fuel imperial America? Or will the American empire go the way of the Leviathans of the past—the Roman, Ottoman, Soviet, and British empires? Can any empire resist the temptation to become drunk with the wine of world power or become intoxicated with the hubris and greed of imperial possibilities? Has not every major empire pursued quixotic dreams of global domination—of shaping the world in its image and for its interest—that resulted in internal decay and doom? Can we committed democrats avert this world-historical pattern and possible fate?

Our fundamental test may lie in our continuing response to 9/11. With the last remnants of the repressive Soviet empire (North Korea and Cuba) proud yet weak, the postimperial European Union in search of an identity and unity, the Asian powers steady but hesitant, and African and Latin American regimes still grappling with postcolonial European and U.S. economic domination, the American empire struts across the globe like a behemoth. We have built up uncontested military might, undeniable cultural power, and transnational corporate and financial hegemony—yet with a huge trade deficit, budget deficit, and intensifying class, racial, religious, and ideological warfare at home. During the cold war, these internal conflicts were often contained by focusing on a common external foe—Communism. Then, for a brief decade, Americans turned on one another in "the culture wars." The well-financed right wing convinced many fellow citizens that the Left—from progressive professors to neoliberal Clintonites, multicultural artists to mainstream feminists, gay and lesbian activists to ecological preservationists—was leading America over the abyss. After 9/11, unity seemed possible—but only if it fit the mold of a narrow patriotism and a revenge-driven lust for a war on terrorism. And as the old-style imperialism of the new hawks in the Bush administration made manifest—through subtle manipulation and outright mendacity—the newly aggressive American empire would not only police the world in light of its interests but also impose its imperial vision and policy—by hook or by crook—on a sleepwalking U.S. citizenry.

Ironically, this vision and policy is, in some ways, continuous with those of earlier administrations that rarely questioned the dogmas of free-market fundamentalism (look at the disaster of Clinton's NAFTA on Canada and Mexico), aggressive militarism (abusive police power in poor communities of color at home), and

escalating authoritarianism (targeted crime fighting and manda-
tory sentencing for incarceration). But the coarse and unabashed
imperial devouring of democracy of the Bush administration is a
low point in America's rocky history of sustaining its still evolving
experiment in democracy. And now instead of Communism as our
external foe we have Islamic terrorism. In addition, the prevailing
conservative culture has made the Left—progressives and liberals—internal enemies. They are considered out of step with the
drumbeat of patriots, who defer to the imperial aims, free-market
policies, cultural conservative views, and personal pieties of the
Bush administration. To put it bluntly, we have reached a rare fork
in the road of American history.

Democracy matters require that we keep track of the intimate
link between domestic issues and foreign policies. Like the empires of old—especially the Roman and British ones—what we do
abroad affects what we can do here and what we do here shapes
what we can do abroad. Probably the most difficult challenge facing our democracy, in the near term at any rate, is that of the cen-
trality of Middle East politics for the American empire. If we are to
stabilize the world and enrich democracy in the world, we must
confront the anti-Semitic hostility of oil-rich autocratic Arab
regimes to Israel's very existence, as well as Israelis' occupation
and subjugation of Palestinian lands and people. We must act more
decisively to stop both the barbaric Palestinian suicide bombers'
murdering of innocent Israeli civilians and the inhumane Israeli
military attacks on unarmed Palestinian refugees. These explosive
issues test the capacity of all Americans to engage in a respectful

and candid dialogue; indeed, they may be pivotal in determining the destiny of American democracy.

How does one honestly criticize the close relationship between American imperial elites and Israeli political officials without falling into ugly anti-Semitic traps? How does one sympathize with the always-fragile existence of a hated people, like the Jews, any-where in the world while also acknowledging that Israel is a mili-tary giant in the Middle East, and that American Jews constitute an organized, powerful force in the American empire to buttress this military might? How does one highlight the inexcusable condi-tions and treatment of Palestinians under Israeli occupation while also acknowledging the aims of some Palestinian groups to push Israel into the sea? Can a Jewish state become a full-fledged secu-lar and democratic state without the annihilation of its Jewish cit-izens? Will the American empire abandon the Jewish state when its economic interests are in direct conflict with such support? Whom are Jews to trust? Whom are Palestinians to trust? Will myopic leadership on both sides preclude any just peace? Will anti-Semitic hatred and anti-Arab bigotry squelch any democratic alternative?

Wrestling with these heart-wrenching queries requires all the critical intelligence and genuine compassion we can muster, yet to remain satisfied with the status quo may well lead to disaster. It is impossible to talk about democracy matters on a global scale with-out engaging these questions. And given the increasing threats of terrorist attacks on America and others abroad, we must grapple with them for our own security and sense of justice.

This does not mean that we should turn away from the wretched

of the earth in Africa facing both the unprecedented AIDS epidemic and the betrayals of authoritarian leaders; or suffering Latin
Americans still under the aegis of transnational corporations and
deferential elected officials; or struggling Asians trying to find or
preserve a niche in the new world order. To focus on the Middle
East is not to single out any regime for special treatment or targeted
demonization. Rather it is to acknowledge that Islamic fundamentalist gangsters do pose a threat to the United States and the world
and that they gain their potency from U.S. foreign policy in the
Middle East. An American imperial response to this real threat
may pose an even greater threat to the United States and the world.
And the American democratic experiment cannot flourish alongside such an American imperial response. This is why the response
of the Bush administration to 9/11 wreaks havoc here and abroad—
more wealth inequality, less resources for jobs, education, health
care, and the arts, and increasing distrust and hatred even from
former allies.

The ugly events of 9/11 should have been an opportunity for national self-scrutiny, In the wake of the shock and horror of those
attacks, many asked the question, why do they hate us? But the
country failed to engage in a serious, sustained, deeply probing examination of the possible answers to that question. Instead, the
leaders of the Bush administration encouraged us to adopt the simplistic and aggressive "with us or against us" stance and we ran
roughshod over our allies, turning a deaf ear to any criticisms of the
course of action the Bush leadership had determined to take. We
have been unwilling—both at this critical juncture and throughout
our history—to turn a sufficiently critical eye on our own behavior

in the world. We have often behaved in an overbearing, imperial, hypocritical manner as we have attained more and more power as a hegemon.

Our hypocritical, bullying behavior in regard to so many of the regions of the world is surely not the only reason for the 9/11 attacks—and it certainly doesn't justify those horribly callous, violent terrorist acts—but we have failed to even consider deeply as a culture the role our imperialist behavior has played in the contempt we have inspired in so much of the world. The Bush administration's abuses of power both at home and in unilaterally invading Iraq and waging a campaign of lies have now provoked an intense scrutiny, and this scrutiny needs to dig deeper than throwing angry barbs at the Bush administration's policies. We've got to reconnect with the energies of a deep democratic tradition in America and reignite them.

If we are to grapple critically with the three antidemocratic dogmas that are raising their ugly heads at this crucial juncture, we will need a more realistic understanding of the crushing ways in which they have operated in the country throughout our history. The first step for any critique of a dogma is to lay bare the history of that dogma—to disclose its contingent origins and ignoble beginnings and to show that the critique of that dogma in history has its own tradition and history. America has a long tradition of excoriating, painful, and powerful critiques of the arrested development of our democracy—critiques of the ravages of our imperial expansionist genocide of the Native Americans; of the crushing of the lives of workers by the callous machinery of capitalist excesses; of the wholesale subjugation of women, gays, and lesbians; and most especially and centrally of the deeply antidemocratic and de-humanizing hypocrisies of white supremacy. This is why the lens of race becomes indispensable in our attempt to understand, preserve, and expand America's democratic experiment.

The brutal atrocities of white supremacy in the American past and present speak volumes about the harsh limits of our democracy over against our professed democratic ideals. Race is the crucial intersecting point where democratic energies clash with American imperial realities in the very making of the grand American experiment of democracy. The voices and viewpoints of reviled and disempowered Amerindians, Asians, Mexicans, Africans, and immigrant Europeans reveal and remind us of the profoundly racist roots of the first American empire—the old America of expansionist Manifest Destiny. How ironic that this New World outpost of the British empire, which rested upon Amerindian lands and was greatly aided by predominantly African enslaved laborers, would institute a grand anti-imperial revolution and embark on a rich democratic experiment?

The contingent origins of American democracy and the ignoble beginnings of imperial America go hand in hand. This dynamic and complex intertwining of racial subjugation and democratic flourishing, of imperial resistance (against the British) and imperial expansion (against Amerindians)—driven primarily by market forces, to satisfy expanding populations and greedy profiteers—sets the stage for the uneven development of the best and worst of American history. We must learn how to keep track of both opposing tendencies if we are to maintain our democratic energy.

Like any other human endeavor, American democracy and imperial America are shot through with multilayered incongruities, contradictions, and imperfect forms of resistance against ugly structures of domination. Race is not a lens to justify sentimental stories of pure heroes of color and impure white villains or melodramatic tales of innocent victims of color and demonic white victimizers. In fact, by shattering such Manichaean (good versus evil/us versus them) views that Americans often tell about themselves, we refuse to simply flip the script and tell new lies about ourselves.

The fight for democracy has ever been one against the oppressive and racist corruptions of empire. To focus solely on electoral politics as the site of democratic life is myopic. Such a focus fails to appreciate the crucial role of the underlying moral commitments and visions and fortifications of the soul that empower and inspire a democratic way of living in the world. These fortifications also fuel deep democratic movements both within the American empire and across the world in global democratic efforts.

The good news in that regard is that there is a deep public reverence for—a love of—democracy in America and a deep democratic tradition. This love of democracy has been most powerfully expressed and pushed forward by our great public intellectuals and artists. Our democratic tradition has built on the profound democratic impulse that stretches all the way back to the Greeks, and this book will, in part, explore the rich insights and expressions of that deep democratic tradition, from the radical iconoclasm of Socrates, to the tragically schizophrenic visions of the American Founding Fathers, to the exuberant and brilliant indictments laid down by hip-hop.

[Three crucial traditions fuel deep democratic energies. The first is the Greek creation of the Socratic commitment to questioning—questioning of ourselves, of authority, of dogma, of parochialism, and of fundamentalism. Vital also is the Jewish invention of the prophetic commitment to justice—for all peoples—formulated in the Hebrew scriptures and echoed in the foundational teachings of Christianity and Islam. And indispensable in addition is the mighty shield and inner strength provided by the tragicomic commitment to hope. The tragicomic is the ability to laugh and retain a sense of life's joy—to preserve hope even while staring in the face of hate and hypocrisy—as against falling into the nihilism of paralyzing despair. This tragicomic hope is expressed in America most profoundly in the wrenchingly honest yet compassionate voices of the black freedom struggle; most poignantly in the painful eloquence of the blues; and most exuberantly in the improvisational virtuosity of jazz.

In the face of elite manipulations and lies, we must draw on the Socratic. The Socratic commitment to questioning requires a relentless self-examination and critique of institutions of authority, motivated by an endless quest for intellectual integrity and moral consistency. It is manifest in a fearless speech—*parrhesia*—that unsettles, unnerves, and unhouses people from their uncritical sleepwalking. As Socrates says in Plato's *Apology*, "Plain speech [*parrhesia*] is the cause of my unpopularity" (24a). His courageous opposition to the seductive yet nihilistic sophists of his day—Greek teachers who employed clever but fallacious arguments—exposed the specious reasoning that legitimated their quest for power and might. His historic effort to unleash painful wisdom seeking—his midwifery of ideas and visions—was predicated on the capacity of all people (such as the brilliant slave boy Meno in the famous dialogue of that name) to engage in a critique of and resistance to the corruptions of mind, soul, and society. We desperately need the deep democratic energy of this Socratic questioning in these times of rampant sophistry on the part of our political elites and their media pundits.

In the face of callous indifference to the suffering wrought by our imperialism, we must draw on the prophetic. The Jewish invention of the prophetic commitment to justice—also central to both Christianity and Islam—is one of the great moral moments in human history. This was the commitment to justice of an oppressed people. It set in motion a prophetic tradition based on the belief that God had imparted this love of justice because God is first and foremost a lover of justice. The Judaic prophetic commitment to justice is therefore predicated on the divine love of justice. Israel— a hated and enslaved people in the most powerful empire of its day (that of Egypt's pharaohs)—is chosen by God because of God's love of justice. And the admonition against inhumane injustice is central to the message of the prophetic: "He who oppresses a poor man insults his maker / He who is kind to the needy honors him" (Proverbs 14:31). Prophetic witness consists of human acts of justice and kindness that attend to the unjust sources of human hurt and misery. Prophetic witness calls attention to the causes of unjustified suffering and unnecessary social misery. It highlights personal and institutional evil, including especially the evil of being indifferent to personal and institutional evil.

Prophetic Judaic figures appeal to us as individuals to join in

transforming the world as communities. They shun individual conversion that precludes collective insurgency. They speak to all peoples and nations to be just and righteous. Amos prophesied not
only to Israel but also to Damascus, Gaza, Tyre, Edom, and Moab—
he spoke in the name of a God who decides the destiny of all nations
(Amos 9:7). Isaiah's domain was addressed to "all you inhabitants
of the world, you who dwell on the earth" (Isaiah 18:3; see also
33:13, 34:1). Jeremiah's calling was that of "a prophet to the nations" (Jeremiah 1:5), including Israel, Ammon, Sidon, and the
other peoples. Hundreds of years before the universalism of Stoic
sages (like Zeno, Cleanthes, and Chrysippus), Judaic prophets
raised the banner of internationalism in the name of divine compassion and divine love of justice. There is nothing tribalistic or
nationalistic about prophetic witness. Xenophobic prejudices and
imperialistic practices are unequivocally condemned. Prophetic
witness has no room for such petty and pernicious inflictions.

Prophetic Judaic figures also target the sole reliance on the force
of power. Aggressive militarism is false security—a mere diversion
from attending to the necessary domestic policies of compassion
that can "heal your wound" (Hosea 5:13). Escalating authoritarianism is a species of injustice that tightens the rope around one's
own neck ("for not by force shall man prevail"; 1 Samuel 2:9). The
deadly charge of idolatry, which is the preeminent weapon in the
prophetic arsenal against injustice, whether that idolatry is the
worship of power or money, sits at the center of prophetic resistance to imperial nations. The golden calf of wealth, along with the
blood-soaked flag that envelops it, is the true idol of empires, past
and present.

This prophetic commitment to justice is foundational in both Christianity and Islam. The gospel of love taught by Jesus and the message of mercy of Muhammad both build on the Jewish invention of the prophetic love of justice. This profound tradition should inform and embolden the struggle against the callous indifference of the plutocratic elites of the American empire about the sufferings of our own poor and oppressed peoples. It should also help to illuminate the effects of our imperialism on the poor and oppressed peoples around the world. Prophetic witness was a driving force in Martin Luther King Jr.'s vision for the civil rights movement, and lay behind the solidarity of Jews and blacks in the enactment of that movement, and it should inform and embolden us in revitalizing our democratic fires.

In the face of cynical and disillusioned acquiescence to the status quo, we must draw on the tragicomic. Tragicomic hope is a profound attitude toward life reflected in the work of artistic geniuses as diverse as Lucian in the Roman empire, Cervantes in the Spanish empire, and Chekhov in the Russian empire. Within the American empire it has been most powerfully expressed in the black invention of the blues in the face of white supremacist powers. As Ralph Ellison wrote in "Richard Wright's Blues," "The blues is an impulse to keep the painful details and episodes of a brutal experience alive in one's aching consciousness, to finger its jagged grain, and to transcend it, not by the consolation of philosophy but by squeezing from it a near-tragic, near-comic lyricism." This powerful blues sensibility—a black interpretation of tragicomic hope open to people of all colors—expresses righteous indignation with a smile and deep inner pain without bitterness or revenge. One finds it in the works of Mark Twain, Tennessee Williams, Eudora Welty, and Thomas Pynchon as well as Bessie Smith, Ma Rainey, Robert Johnson, and Leroy Carr.

There are a number of white lovers of the blues who have a tragicomic sensibility, but for too many in white America the blues remains a kind of exotic source of amusement, a kind of primitivistic occasion for entertainment only. The blues is not simply a music to titillate; it is a hard-fought way of life, and as such it should unsettle and unnerve whites about the legacy of white supremacy. The blues is relevant today because when we look down through the corridors of time, the black American interpretation of tragicomic hope in the face of dehumanizing hate and oppression will be seen as the only kind of hope that has any kind of maturity in a world of overwhelming barbarity and bestiality. That barbarity is found not just in the form of terrorism but in the form of the emptiness of our lives—in terms of the wasted human potential that we see around the world. In this sense, the blues is a great democratic contribution of black people to world history.

The ugly terrorist attacks on innocent civilians on 9/11 plunged the whole country into the blues. Never before have Americans of *all* classes, colors, regions, religions, genders, and sexual orientations felt unsafe, unprotected, subject to random violence, and hated. Yet to have been designated and treated as a nigger in America for over 350 years has been to feel unsafe, unprotected, subject to random violence, and hated. The high point of the black response to American terrorism (or niggerization) is found in the compassionate and courageous voice of Emmett Till's mother, who stepped up to the lectern at Pilgrim Baptist Church in Chicago in

1955 at the funeral of her fourteen-year-old son, after his murder by American terrorists, and said: "I don't have a minute to hate. I'll pursue justice for the rest of my life." And that is precisely what Mamie Till Mobley did until her death in 2003. Her commitment to justice had nothing to do with naïveté. When Mississippi officials tried to keep any images of Emmett's brutalized body out of the press—his head had swollen to five times its normal size—Mamie Till Mobley held an open-casket service for all the world to see. That is the essence of the blues: to stare painful truths in the face and persevere without cynicism or pessimism.

Much of the future of democracy in America and the world hangs on grasping and preserving the rich democratic tradition that produced the Douglasses, Kings, Coltranes, and Mobleys in the face of terrorist attacks and cowardly assaults. Since 9/11 we have experienced the niggerization of America, and as we struggle against the imperialistic arrogance of the us-versus-them, revenge-driven policies of the Bush administration, we as a blues nation must learn from a blues people how to keep alive our deep democratic energies in dark times rather than resort to the tempting and easier response of militarism and authoritarianism.

No democracy can flourish against the corruptions of plutocratic, imperial forces—or withstand the temptations of militarism in the face of terrorist hate—without a citizenry girded by these three moral pillars of Socratic questioning, prophetic witness, and tragicomic hope. The hawks and proselytizers of the Bush administration have professed themselves to be the guardians of American democracy, but there is a deep democratic tradition in this country that speaks powerfully against their nihilistic, antidemocratic abuse of power and that can fortify genuine democrats today in the fight against imperialism. That democratic fervor is found in the beacon calls for imaginative self-creation in Ralph Waldo Emerson, in the dark warnings of imminent self-destruction in Herman Melville, in the impassioned odes to democratic possibility in Walt Whitman. It is found most urgently and poignantly in the prophetic and powerful voices of the long black freedom struggle—from the democratic eloquence of Frederick Douglass to the soaring civic sermons of Martin Luther King Jr., in the wrenching artistic honesty of James Baldwin and Toni Morrison, and in the expressive force and improvisatory genius of the blues/jazz tradition, all forged in the night side of America and defying the demeaning strictures of white supremacy. The greatest intellectual, moral, political, and spiritual resources in America that may renew the soul and preserve the future of American democracy reside in this multiracial, rich democratic heritage.

Let us not be deceived: the great dramatic battle of the twenty-first century is the dismantling of empire and the deepening of democracy. This is as much or more a colossal fight over visions and ideas as a catastrophic struggle over profits and missiles. Globalization is inescapable—the question is whether it will be a democratic globalization or a U.S.-led corporate globalization (with thin democratic rhetoric). This is why what we think, how we care, and the way we fight mean so much now in democracy matters. We live in a propitious yet perilous moment in which it has become fashionable to celebrate the benefits of imperial rule and acceptable to condone the decline of democratic governance. The pervasive climate of opinion and the prevailing culture of consumption make it difficult for us to even imagine the revival of the deep democratizing energies of our past and conceive of making real progress in the fight against imperialism.

But we must remember that the basis of democratic leadership is ordinary citizens' desire to take their country back from the hands of corrupted plutocratic and imperial elites. This desire is predicated on an awakening among the populace from the seductive lies and comforting illusions that sedate them and a moral channeling of new political energy that constitutes a formidable threat to the status quo. This is what happened in the 1860s, 1890s, 1930s, and 1960s in American history. Just as it looked as if we were about to lose the American democratic experiment—in the face of civil war, imperial greed, economic depression, and racial upheaval—in each of these periods a democratic awakening and activistic energy emerged to keep our democratic project afloat. We must work and hope for such an awakening once again.

2

NIHILISM IN AMERICA

I muse upon my country's ills—
    The tempest bursting from the waste of Time
On the world's fairest hope linked with man's foulest crime.

    —HERMAN MELVILLE, "Misgivings" (1860)

    Power unanointed may come—
Dominion (unsought by the free)
    And the Iron Dome,
Stronger for stress and strain,
Fling her huge shadow athwart the main;
But the founders' dream shall flee.

    —HERMAN MELVILLE, "The Conflict of Convictions" (1860–61)

The evolution that saw electoral politics become assimilated to the practices of the market place—candidates marketed as products, elections reduced to slogans and advertisements, voters maneuvered into the position where caveat emptor becomes their most reliable guide—suggests a conclusion, that postmodern despotism consists of the collapse of politics into economics and the emergence of a new form, the economic polity. The regime is, as Tocqueville suggested, benign, power transmuted into solicitude, popular sovereignty into consumerism, mutuality into mutual funds, and the democracy of citizens into shareholder democracy.

—SHELDON S. WOLIN, "Postdemocracy,"
Tocqueville Between Two Worlds (2001)

The most frightening feature of imperial America is neither the myopic mendaciousness of the Republican Party nor the pathetic spinelessness of the Democratic Party (though the Democratic spine has been stiffening in response to the egregious excesses of Bush). Instead, what is most terrifying—including the perennial threat of cowardly terrorists—is the insidious growth of *deadening nihilisms* across political lines, nihilisms that have been suffocating the deep democratic energies in America. In *Race Matters*, I examined the increasing nihilism in black America as the "lived experience of coping with a life of horrifying meaningless-ness, hopelessness, and (most important) lovelessness." This monumental collapse of meaning, hope, and love primarily resulted from "the saturation of market forces and market moralities in black life and the present crisis of black leadership." Families bereft of resources and communities devoid of webs of care yield thin cul-tural armor against the demons of despair, dread, and disappoint-ment. Nihilistic criminal thugs often step into the void and rule a brutal underground economy and frightened community, and timid black leaders offer no energizing vision to perishing people.

Needless to say, nihilism is not confined to black America. Psychic depression, personal worthlessness, and social despair are widespread in America as a whole. The vast majority of citizens—struggling to preserve a livelihood, raise children, and live decent lives—are disillusioned with social forces that seem beyond their control. Just as in the black community, the saturation of market forces in American life generates a market morality that undermines a sense of meaning and larger purpose. The dogma of free-market fundamentalism has run amok, and the pursuit of profits by any legal (or illegal) means—with little or no public accountability—guides the behavior of the most powerful and influential institutions in our lives: transnational corporations. And yet corporate elites are not fully in control of market forces even as they try to bend them to their own benefit. Their frantic race to the bottom line indeed lifts some boats yet it often pollutes the water and empties out the democratic energies necessary to guide the ship of state. In fact, it leaves the ship of state devoid of vital public trust and a common sense of destiny.

The perception of pervasive corruption at the top seems to many to justify the unprincipled quest to succeed at any cost in their own lives, and the widespread cheating in our culture reflects this sad truth. The oppressive effect of the prevailing market moralities leads to a form of sleepwalking from womb to tomb, with the majority of citizens content to focus on private careers and be distracted with stimulating amusements. They have given up any real hope of shaping the collective destiny of the nation. Sour cynicism, political apathy, and cultural escapism become the pervasive options.

The public has good cause for disillusionment with the American democratic system. The saturation of market forces and market moralities has indeed corrupted our system all the way up. Our leadership elite have themselves lost faith in the efficacy of adhering to democratic principles in the face of the overwhelming power of those market forces. They are caught up in the corrupting influences of market morality. Our politicians have sacrificed their principles on the altar of special interests; our corporate leaders have sacrificed their integrity on the altar of profits; and our media watchdogs have sacrificed the voice of dissent on the altar of audience competition.

Our leadership elite may still *want* to believe in democratic principles—they certainly profess that they do—but in practice they have shown themselves all too willing to violate those principles in order to gain or retain power. The flip side of the nihilism of despair is this nihilism of the unprincipled abuse of power. When the lack of belief in the power of principles prevails, the void is filled by the will to power of the market, by the drive to succeed at the cost of others rather than the drive to decency and integrity. In the poverty-stricken inner cities, this nihilism leads to street gangsterism, and in the halls of elite power it leads to elite gangsterism, which I will call *political* nihilism.

Despite their religious rhetoric and patriotic utterances— habitual gestures they enact ad nauseam—most American politicians have succumbed to what they deem the necessary evils of market corruptions. Serious commitment to truth, integrity, and principle gives way to mendacity, manipulation, and misinformation in the increasingly unprincipled political marketplace. Political nihilism now sets the tone for public discourse, and market moralities now dictate the landscape of a stifled American democracy. Market research (polling) all too often takes the place of principled problem solving; appealing lies take the place of uncomfortable truths; backroom deals take the place of public debate. The broad array of citizens' voices is channeled through a narrow tunnel of market-driven mass-media outlets, grossly limiting the public presentation of popular sentiment. There are in fact impassioned voices of dissent, often expressed with special fervor through the marvelously democratic medium of the Web. There has been a massive outpouring of moral outrage at Bush, which is a promising sign of the renewal of the spirit of democratic discourse. But the censorship of the market is insidious.

American democracy has always been premised on a capitalist, market-driven economy of prosperity, and just as our capitalism has always been subject to antidemocratic corruptions and has shut out so many from the fruits of prosperity, our political system has in turn been subject to capitalist corruptions. The hallmark of political nihilism is the public appeal to fear and greed, and too much of American politics today has been reduced to such vulgar appeals. Just so, Bush promoted his irresponsible tax cuts by offering the largely chimerical promise of a child-tax rebate, and promoted his repressive Patriot Act by appealing to the fear of terrorism. A political nihilist is one who is not simply intoxicated with the exercise of power but also obsessed with stifling any criticism of that exercise of power. He will use clever arguments to rationalize his will to power and deploy skillful strategies, denying the pain and suffering he may cause, in order to shape the world and control history in light of the pursuit of power. The word *nihilism* may seem strong, but we saw President Johnson do this with claims about the Gulf of Tonkin for the Vietnam War and President Bush do this with claims about weapons of mass destruction in the invasion of Iraq.

As a consequence of nihilistic corruptions, the reverence for, faith in, and deep commitment to democracy are so undermined in America today that there is not only a disillusionment with our politicians but also a loss of belief for too many people in the efficacy of government altogether, and in the honesty of corporate America as a whole. Yet many citizens still yearn to hear authentic expressions of democratic values and to believe that policies being pursued are for the public good, not narrowly serving electoral purposes or elite interests.

We are suffering in America today from three particular forms of political nihilism, each with its own false justifications and vicious consequences: evangelical nihilism, paternalistic nihilism, and sentimental nihilism. The classic expression of *evangelical* nihilism is found in Plato's *Republic* in the person of Thrasymachus, the Sophist who argues with Socrates that might makes right. Thrasymachus mocks truth, integrity, and principle by claiming that power, might, and force dictate desirable political action and public policy. Raw power rather than moral principles determines what is right. For him, the terms of what is just must be dictated by imperial elites because such exercise of power is necessary in order to ensure national security and prosperity. In true evangelical spirit, such nihilists tend to become militant, broaching no dissenting views. The fundamental mission of Socratic questioning is, in fact, to show that this militance is morally wrong and spiritually empty.

In this way, the movers and shakers in the Republican Party—and especially the hawks in the Bush administration—are not simply conservative elites and right-wing ideologues. More pointedly, they are *evangelical nihilists*, drunk with power and driven by grand delusions of American domination of the world. And they have been willing to lie and to abuse their control of American power in order to pursue that dominance. Unlike their idol, Ronald Reagan—a masterful conservative communicator and true believer in the rightness of America's might—the new hawks seem to believe that America's might actually determines what is right. In this tradition of thinking, we wouldn't be so powerful if we weren't right, so our might shows that we are right. Accordingly, America's power justifies the refusal to listen to or reply to our critics, be they former allies in the United Nations or fellow citizens of goodwill demonstrating in the streets. America's hubris means only that our power moves must be forms of empowerment for others. What we do must be a force for good for others, even if others disagree, dissent, or even are harmed. President Bush and his inner circle have acted like exemplary evangelical nihilists—present-day Thrasymachuses—who show no respect for Socratic questioning of their positions and actions. They even characterize such questioning as unpatriotic.

Yet the present reality of political nihilism is not so simple as that of the evangelical nihilistic arrogance of the Bush administration. There is political nihilism to be found within the ranks of the Democratic Party as well, in the form of *paternalistic* nihilism. The canonical articulation of paternalistic nihilism is put forward in Fyodor Dostoyevsky's *The Brothers Karamazov* in the character of the Grand Inquisitor, a terribly disillusioned priest in the city of Seville during the time of the Spanish Inquisition. So cynical has the Grand Inquisitor become that although he knows the abuses of the Inquisition are a horrible perversion of the teachings of Christ, perpetrated by a terribly corrupted church, he nevertheless takes part in those abuses—condemning many supposed infidels to death. He has come to believe that the corrupted church is the best that mankind can hope for because human society is simply not capable of living in the way Christ instructed. We are not capable of achieving the world of equality, humility, and compassionate caring that He instructed mankind to strive for. Better not to rock the boat with pipe dreams of a radical transformation of society. The elite of the church can do more good, the Inquisitor believes, by working within the corrupted system, paternally deceiving the public, shielding society from the terrible burden of the mandates of truth. He has cast his lot with corruption.

The elites in the Democratic Party—especially in the Senate and the House—are not only liberal and centrist supporters of social equality and individual freedoms; more pointedly they are *paternalistic nihilists* who have become ineffectual by having bought into the corruptions of the power-hungry system. Though they may wish that the system could be made to serve more truly democratic purposes, they have succumbed to the belief that a more radical fight for a truer democracy, battling against the corruption of elites, is largely futile. So they've joined the game in the delusional belief that at least they are doing so in the better interests of the public. Needless to say, they have much more to offer than Republicans, especially President Bush and his chief political strategist, Karl Rove, *and they will play an indispensable role in the crucial anti-Bush united front needed to revitalize American democracy.* Yet they are still more part of the problem than the solution to our impasse.

The paternalistic nihilistic view that much good can be done by working within the corrupted system is not altogether misguided. The greatest Democratic legislation—that of the New Deal and of the Great Society—was passed due to skillful mastering of the system. But the present Democratic Party has lost its footing in terms of its foundational mission to fight the plutocracy. Corporate elites in the American empire have always cast a dark shadow over the operations of power in American government. And although these elites are mighty, they are not almighty. The Democratic Party leaders seem to have lost the conviction that corporate elites can be forced to make concessions under the pressure of organized democratic forces. But our history has shown they can be forced. The key reason women could not vote until 1920, indigenous peoples until 1924, and most blacks until 1964 was that they could not bring organized democratic pressures to bear in order to limit the power of wealthy white male citizens. Yet, when they marshaled that organized force, they got the vote.

For most of the history of the American empire, government has been a tool for preserving and furthering the power and might of white male corporate elites—a small percentage of white men in the country. The uniqueness of Franklin Delano Roosevelt was his determination to oppose this power and might—a vision and courage that far exceeded those of his earlier progressive precursors Theodore Roosevelt and Woodrow Wilson. It is no accident that FDR is so vehemently hated by the evangelical nihilistic elites of the present-day empire. The uniqueness of Lyndon Johnson was that he recognized that the interests of poor whites were the same as those of the vast majority of black people in America, a view suggested by Michael Harrington's classic *The Other America* (1962).

The achievements of Roosevelt and Johnson are salutary precisely because they promoted the democratic, not the plutocratic, tendency in the American empire. And they did so primarily because of organized pressure from the labor movement under Roosevelt and the black and gray movements under Johnson.

The example and legacy of FDR in the 1930s and early 1940s and of Johnson in the 1960s are the high moments of democratic and Democratic Party electoral politics in the United States, proving that the American government can side with working and poor people, and even with black people, within the context of empire. Under Roosevelt the organized power of working people was made legitimate, and under Johnson one-half of all black people and elderly citizens (of all colors) were lifted out of poverty. These achievements—resulting from intense organized struggle—may feel so far away, in both time and possibility, that holding them up as models may seem pointless. But reclaiming this powerful democratic legacy is precisely the mission before the Democratic Party today. An essential element in achieving this renewal will be for the party to become more genuinely responsive to black concerns—understanding them not as matters of a "special interest" but as being in the public interest. This would lead to a strengthening of both the moral and the electoral force of the party. As Michael Dawson wrote so trenchantly in his *Black Visions: The Roots of Contemporary African-American Political Ideologies* (2001):

> What should not seem surprising is that at the turn of the century African Americans continue to believe that American democracy is broken—and the 2000

presidential elections did nothing to convince blacks
that the nation was on the road to recovery. African
Americans are still waiting for black visions of a just
and egalitarian society to become American visions.
It increasingly is clear, though, that many African
Americans fear that Malcolm X was right when he
worried that blacks held a vision of freedom larger
than America is prepared to accept.

The Democratic Party elites are too often unwilling to tell the
American people just how connected they and their Republican
colleagues are to powerful corporations and influential lobbyists.
Their caving in to Bush's Iraq war, and their support for the loosening of regulations on corporations that led to the recent wave of
scandals, are two blatant examples. In these legislative votes, most
Democrats failed to follow their conscience, following instead the
polls and their reelection strategies. Unlike their idol, Bill
Clinton—a masterful neoliberal communicator who subordinated
his conscience to the exigencies of reelection strategies, but was
able to conceal his opportunism with his charisma—the vast majority of Democratic Party elites are rendered impotent by their
timidity and paralyzed by their cupidity (their courting of corporate
donors). Their unprincipled compromises reinforce the idea that
corporate influence and lobbyists' clout run the U.S. government.

Senators Hillary Clinton and John Kerry are exemplary paternalistic nihilists—contemporary Grand Inquisitors who long to believe in a grand democratic vision yet cannot manage to speak with
full candor or attack the corruptions of the system at their heart. So

they defer to pollsters, lobbyists, and powerful corporate interests even as they espouse populist rhetoric and democratic concerns. Their centrist or conservative policies on welfare reform, the Iraq war, and justice in the Israeli-Palestinian conflict speak volumes— they are opportunistic efforts to satisfy centrist or conservative constituencies. In this way, both follow the lead of Bill Clinton. Inadvertently, they contribute to the conservative drift of the country heralded by Republicans.

The political nihilism in America today is not limited to the arena of party politics; it has infiltrated our media culture as well in the form of *sentimental* nihilism. While an essential mission of the news organizations in a democracy should be to expose the lies and manipulations of our political and economic leaders—and surely many media watchdogs devote themselves to that task—too much of what passes for news today is really a form of entertainment. So many shows follow a crude formula for providing titillating coverage that masks itself as news. Those who are purveyors of this bastardized form of reporting are *sentimental nihilists*, willing to sidestep or even bludgeon the truth or unpleasant and unpopular facts and stories, in order to provide an emotionally satisfying show. This is the dominance of sentiment over truth telling in order to build up market share. Our market-driven media have become much too constrained in the coverage of unpleasant truths, much too preoccupied with the concerns and views of middle-class and upper-class white people, and much too beholden to the political persuasions of the media moguls.

Hence we have witnessed the breakdown in media ethics—going after "good" stories even if the truth has to be stretched or outright fabrications are condoned. The overwhelming dominance of market-driven pressures has also led to the outburst of blatantly partisan punditry. And even the supposed do-gooders in the media often limit the depth of their analysis and the range of their truth telling so as not to offend advertisers and mainstream opinion.

There is a vibrant upswing in alternative coverage due to the Web, with so many Weblogs on issues getting a wider range of perspectives out—though some go too far into crude advocacy the other way. There are also still many quality reporters who have developed enough of a reputation and following to write harder-hitting pieces, and there are specialty periodicals that offer substantive, analytical reporting. But our mass media are dominated by the ambulance chasers and the blatantly partisan hacks, mostly on the right. Many newspeople are deep believers in the principle of the free press and the special role it's meant to play in our democracy, and yet that belief all too often amounts to sentiment because they fail to act more consistently on that principle.

The most powerful depiction of such principled sentimental nihilism in recent times that I know of is presented in Toni Morrison's novel *Beloved*, represented by the family of the Bodwins. Mr. and Mrs. Bodwin, a white brother and sister, are abolitionists who have helped a number of slaves gain their freedom. But in conversations during the course of the novel, they betray the limits of their commitment to racial equality and of their courage to fight for it. They enjoy their comfortable lives, and though they see themselves as bleeding hearts who abhor the evil of slavery, they refuse to speak of the true depths of its horrors to their fellow white citizens, and even to the former slaves they helped to freedom. They know full well about slavery's venality, but they lack the courage to exercise frank and plain speech against it because they fear social shunning. Such cowardly lack of willingness to engage in truth telling, even at the cost of social ills, is the fundamental characteristic of sentimental nihilism.

So many of our mainstream media pundits—from neoliberals to the Far Right—are sentimental nihilists. They are aware of the corrupt links of the mass media to corporate interests and government, yet they fail to speak out clearly or consistently against that corruption. Though our cultural mythology has promoted the notion of "fair and balanced" coverage and impartiality, our news organizations have always been more partisanly political than the ideal and have always been subject to market pressures. Yet we now have a media whose vulgar partisanship is corrupting our public life. Those who engage in biased reporting reinforce the deep polarization and balkanization of the citizenry and contribute much to the decline of public trust in meaningful political conversation. The relentless pursuit of power among the media elite—in the form of ratings and market share—is indulged in with little regard for the consequences for our democracy.

While the right-wing pundits are overt in their superficial pandering, the more subtle and insidious constraints on hard-hitting, truthful reporting are at least as troubling. The bombastic carnival barkers are relatively easy to expose in their sentimental manipulations. The more principled believers in the special role of a balanced and free press, who all too frequently bow to market pressures, are a more serious threat.

Sentimental nihilism is content to remain on the surface of

problems rather than pursue their substantive depths. It pays simplistic lip service to issues rather than portraying their complexity. This sad display of highly ambitious yet too often docile and deferential newspeople preoccupied with a market bottom line has not been lost on the public and has contributed to the widespread public apathy about our politics. Yet the hard-hitting, deeply probing periodicals and shows that do exist struggle for market share because the allure of the entertainment offered by the mass-appeal versions is so strong. Most significantly, the obsessive touting of dubious statistics and sound bites by mainstream pundits points citizens away from a true reckoning with the institutional causes of social misery.

Democracy depends, in large part, on a free and frank press willing to speak painful truths to the public about our society, including the fact of their own complicity in superficiality and simplistic reportage. There can be no democratic *paideia*—the critical cultivation of an active citizenry—without democratic *parrhesia*—a bold and courageous press willing to speak against the misinformation and mendacities of elites. Democracy matters are in peril when the so-called free press lacks the autonomy or courage to inspire democratic energies.

These pervasive nihilisms in American democracy today have made way for a resurgent imperialism—the ultimate expression of the market-driven grasp for power. The nihilistic market-dominated mentality—the quest for wealth and power—leads to the drive for conquest, and it's when market morality prevails over democratic principle that imperialism reigns supreme. Market-obsessed nihilism—the corporation as the embodiment of absolute will—is the Achilles' heel of American democracy that parades as its crown jewel. Free-market fundamentalism has for so long been the precondition of American democracy that we have rendered it sacred—an unexamined fetish that we worship.

These three nihilistic threats connect the spiritual to the social, the personal to the political, and the existential to the economic. They shape every dimension of our lives, from the bedroom to the corporate meeting room, from street to suite. Serious reflection on democracy matters is always more than a view about the next election. It also forces us to think broadly about the future of the American Republic, and the overriding issue we must grapple with in the post-9/11 world is the threat of this rising imperialism. The pervasive nihilism of our political culture and this surging imperialism go hand in hand. The imperialist impulse does not fully define us, but it has a long and brutal history that we must confront. If we want to understand this imperialist nihilism that runs so deep in our culture, we should start by looking at its history, and to do that we must start with race. The pursuit of empire and racist oppressions and exclusions have been intimately interlinked.

Indigenous peoples, Mexican peasants, Asian laborers, and especially African slaves have wrestled with forms of antidemocratic nihilism in America unknown to most European immigrants—even given their heroic struggles against harsh prejudice in America. Anti-Semitism, anti-Catholicism, and antiunionism indeed have been ugly in American history. But the vicious legacy of white supremacy has inflicted deeper wounds on the American landscape. These deep wounds provide a profound lens—they yield painful truths about the limits of democracy in America.

The American democratic experiment is unique in human history not because we are God's chosen people to lead the world, nor because we are always a force for good in the world, but because of our refusal to acknowledge the deeply racist and imperial roots of our democratic project. We are exceptional because of our denial of the antidemocratic foundation stones of American democracy. No other democratic nation revels so blatantly in such self-deceptive innocence, such self-paralyzing reluctance to confront the nightside of its own history. This sentimental flight from history—or adolescent escape from painful truths about ourselves—means that even as we grow old, grow big, and grow powerful, we have yet to grow up. To confront the role of race and empire is to grapple with what we would like to avoid, but we avoid that confrontation at the risk of our democratic maturation. To delve into our legacy of race and empire is to unleash our often-untapped democratic energies of Socratic questioning, prophetic witness, and tragicomic hope.

To engage in this Socratic questioning of America is not to trash our country, but rather to tease out those traditions in our history that enable us to wrestle with difficult realities we often deny. The aim of this Socratic questioning is democratic *paideia*—the cultivation of an active, informed citizenry—in order to preserve and deepen our democratic experiment. Race has always been the crucial litmus test for such maturity in America. To acknowledge the deeply racist and imperial roots of our democratic project is anti-American only if one holds to a childish belief that America is pure and pristine, or if one opts for self-destructive nihilistic rationalizations. One of our most crucial tasks now as democrats is to expose and extricate the antidemocratic impulses within our democracy. It is when we confront the challenges of our anti-democratic inclinations as a country that our most profound democratic commitments are born, both on the individual and on the societal level. Only the nihilists among us tremble in their boots at such a prospect.

In examining the deep roots of imperialism in American history, it is important to know that most of the grand democratic projects in human history—from Athens to America—have xenophobic and imperial roots. The most famous of all speeches in democratic Athens—Pericles' great funeral oration rendered in Thucydides' classic *History of the Peloponnesian War*—celebrated democracy at home while glorifying Athens's imperial domination of other peoples abroad. "For Athens alone of her contemporaries," Pericles proclaimed, "is found when tested to be greater than her reputation . . . we have forced every sea and land to be the highway of our daring, and everywhere, whether for evil or for good, have left imperishable monuments behind us." Even the democracy at home he lauded was seriously compromised, rooted as it was in slavery, patriarchal households, and the economic advantage of the cheap labor of resident aliens (like the great Aristotle) who could not vote. Similarly, the democratic experiments of Rome, France, England, and Germany had deep imperial foundations.

The fundamental paradox of American democracy in particular is that it gallantly emerged as a fragile democratic experiment over and against an oppressive British empire—and aided by the French and Dutch empires—even while harboring its own imperial visions of westward expansion, with more than 20 percent of its population consisting of enslaved Africans. In short, we are a democracy of rebels who nonetheless re-created in our own new nation many of the oppressions we had rebelled against. The Declaration of Independence, principally written by the thirty-three-year-old revolutionary Thomas Jefferson—who himself embodied this paradox, being both a courageous freedom fighter against British imperialism and a cowardly aristocratic slaveholder of hundreds of Africans in his beloved Virginia—offers telling testament to this complex and contradictory character of the American democratic experiment.

The reference in the Declaration to indigenous peoples as "Savages" worthy of American expansionist domination for an "empire of liberty" further reveals this contradiction. In listing the colonies' charges against British oppression, Jefferson sounds this theme in his last charge: "He [the British oppressor] has excited domestic insurrections amongst us, and has endeavoured to bring on the inhabitants of our frontiers, the merciless Indian Savages, whose known rule of warfare, is an undistinguished destruction of all ages, sexes and conditions." A few years after he wrote the Declaration, Jefferson proclaimed that he trembled for his country when he thought of the suffering of slaves and that God was just—a suffering that he was all too aware enabled his political career, since his slavocratic views were so popular with his constituencies, and a suffering he intimately and directly contributed to in a mighty way in both public policy and personal behavior. Yet in 1783, less than a decade after Jefferson's Declaration, the chief justice in Massachusetts declared an end to slavery in his state because "a different idea has taken place with the people of America" in which "all men are born free and equal" that is "totally repugnant to the idea of being born slaves."

George Washington wrestled with this tension on the battlefield for his country and within his soul. With his victorious Continental army at Yorktown 25 percent black, he struggled to shed some of his slaveholder's mentality, ultimately freeing his slaves at his death. He warned his countrymen about getting involved in the imperial affairs and wars of Europe, yet he acknowledged that the future of the young democratic republic rested on westward expansion and imperial subjugation of indigenous peoples. In 1787 Benjamin Franklin, in his closing speech at the Constitutional Convention, uttered a dreadful warning that America would likely end up as a despotic republic with docile citizens:

> I agree to this constitution with all its faults, if they are such: because I think a general government necessary for us, and there is no form of government but what may be a blessing to the people if well-administered; and I believe farther that this is likely to be well administered for a Course of Years and can only end in Despotism as other forms have done before it, when the People shall become so corrupted as to need Despotic Government, being incapable of any other.

From the birth of American democracy, then, the battle was raging over the scope of freedom, the reach of equality, and the tension between democratic and xenophobic elements.

The most painful truth in the making of America—a truth that shatters all pretensions to innocence and undercuts all efforts of denial—is that *the enslavement of Africans and the imperial expansion over indigenous peoples and their lands were undeniable preconditions for the possibility of American democracy.* There could be no such thing as an experiment in American democracy without these racist and imperial foundations. It is no accident that from the nation's founding (1789) to the Civil War (1861) the vast majority of Supreme Court justices—the highest rule of law in the land—were slaveholders and imperial expansionists. And for forty-nine of these seventy-two years, the presidency of the United States was held by slaveholders and imperial expansionists. And the only ones reelected president were slaveholders and imperial expansionists.

The most powerful and poignant work ever written about America—Alexis de Tocqueville's classic two-volume *Democracy in America* (1835, 1840)—reached a number of dark conclusions about this lethal mix of race, empire, and democracy. Tocqueville feared that America would produce a new form of despotism in the world—a democratic despotism, a term also used by W. E. B. Du Bois almost one hundred years later. This despotism would be guilty of genocide against indigenous peoples and unable to create a multiracial democracy owing to the deep white supremacist practices of the country's tyrannical majority. The last and longest chapter of Tocqueville's first volume—a chapter often skipped over or treated lightly by scholars who fan and fuel America's denial of its racist and imperial roots—put forward the most difficult and delicate challenge to the American democratic experiment: would race and empire undermine American democracy?

I do not imagine that the white and black races will ever live in any country upon an equal footing. But I believe the difficulty to be still greater in the United States than elsewhere. An isolated individual may surmount the prejudices of religion, of his country, or of his race, and if this individual is a king he may effect surprising changes in society; but a whole people cannot rise, as it were, above itself. A despot who should subject the Americans and their former slaves to the same yoke, might perhaps succeed in commingling their races; but as long as the American democracy remains at the head of affairs, no one will undertake so difficult a task; and it may be foreseen that the freer the white population of the United States becomes, the more isolated will it remain. . . .

If ever America undergoes great revolutions, they will be brought about by the presence of the black race on the soil of the United States,—that is to say, they will owe their origin, not to the equality, but to the inequality, of conditions.

The prophetic astuteness of Tocqueville's critique is sometimes attributed in part to his outsider status, and yet powerful voices from within the country, both the famous and the largely forgotten, expressed the same fears of the ultimate consequences of racism and imperialism earlier. Their words speak more powerfully than we can today about the menacing nature of these twin forces as the country wrestled with the paradoxes implicit in its founding. The free black man David Walker and the white abolitionist Lydia Maria Child—two public intellectuals in the grand democratic tradition—had already raised Tocqueville's explosive question. In 1829 Walker published his excoriating *Appeal to the Colored Citizens of the World*, a work banned in much of America and the cause of his murder in 1830. Highlighting Thomas Jefferson's hypocrisy as the author of the Declaration who also, in his notorious *Notes on the State of Virginia*, put forth a degrading analysis of the inferiority of African Americans, Walker wrote:

> Has Mr. Jefferson declared to the world, that we are inferior to whites, both in the endowments of our bodies and our minds? It is indeed surprising that a man of such great learning, combined with such excellent natural parts, should speak so of a set of men in chains. . . .
>
> Do you know that Mr. Jefferson was one of as great characters as ever lived among the whites? See his writings for the world, and public labours for the United States of America. Do you believe that the assertions of such a man, will pass away into oblivion unobserved by this people and the world? If you do you are much-mistaken. See how the American people treat us—have we souls in our bodies? . . .
>
> See your Declaration Americans! ! ! Do you understand your own language? Hear your language, proclaimed to the world, July 4th, 1776—"We hold

these truths to be self evident—that ALL MEN ARE
CREATED EQUAL!"

Child, a radical abolitionist, admonished the country about the
evils of slavery in 1833 with her *An Appeal in Favor of That Class of
Americans Called Africans:*

> I am fully aware of the unpopularity of the task I have
> undertaken; but though I *expect* ridicule and cen-
> sure, I cannot *fear* them. . . .
>
> Should it be the means of advancing, even one sin-
> gle hour, the inevitable progress of truth and justice,
> I would not exchange the consciousness for all Roths-
> child's wealth, or Sir Walter's fame.
>
> Who does not see that the American people are
> walking over a subterranean fire, the flames of which
> are fed by slavery?

The greatest novel ever written by an American, *Moby-Dick*
(1851), is the thirty-two-year-old Herman Melville's scathing exploration of the evils of nihilistic imperialist power, a power he
recognized and abhorred at the heart of the American character.
Melville was a staunch antiracist, anti-imperialist, and lover of
democracy—ironically, his father-in-law was the judge who sustained the vicious Fugitive Slave Act that was a catalyst for the Civil
War—and *Moby-Dick* can be read, in part, as a commentary on the
ills of American democracy. The nihilist Ahab, drunk with power
and the crazed embodiment of an absolute will to dominate and

conquer—fueled largely by wounded ego and worldly pride—leads his multiracial crew into the abyss of history, with the fetish of whiteness dangling before him.

The greatness of Abraham Lincoln was his courage to confront publicly the nightside of American democracy through deep Socratic questioning, unfailing prophetic love of justice, and excruciating tragicomic hope for a "more perfect union," even in the midst of the white supremacist hurricane that nearly wiped the American democratic experiment off the map. Despite his distance from fervid abolitionists, his authoritarian lifting of habeas corpus during the Civil War, and his reluctance to embrace multiracial democracy, Lincoln exemplifies the integrity of democratic energy. He knew that democratic experiments require not only courageous truth telling but also practical wisdom. Lincoln was morally opposed to slavery, yet the decision to free the slaves (though those in the Confederate South only) was nonetheless a herculean battle for him. That battle in itself is emblematic of the horrible intertwining of democracy, race, and empire at the core of the nation. He knew all too well the fragility of the support for the Union cause among key border states and that freeing the slaves would likely throw them over to the Confederacy, and so his love of the American democratic experiment caught him in a horrible irony that required him to condone the most antidemocratic of American practices.

Only when he realized that the influx of over 150,000 black soldiers would be pivotal in saving the Union did he issue his Emancipation Proclamation, which then led him to support the New Orleans plan of multiracial voting—a decision directly responsible for his assassination by the white supremacist John Wilkes Booth. His three-minute Second Inaugural Address is the most profound expression of Socratic questioning, prophetic witness, and tragicomic hope ever uttered by an American president, revealing what serious wrestling with the implications of racism and empire can bring out of those who have a passion for democracy matters:

> Fondly do we hope, fervently do we pray, that this mighty scourge of war may speedily pass away. Yet, if God wills that it continue, until all the wealth piled by the bondsman's two hundred and fifty years of unrequited toil shall be sunk, and until every drop of blood drawn with the lash, shall be paid by another drawn with the sword, as was said three thousand years ago, so still it must be said "the judgments of the Lord are true and righteous altogether."

Ironically, immediately following the war, the U.S. government would deploy troops in the imperialist cause of further westward expansion, engaging in a genocidal war against the indigenous peoples. And after the brief twelve-year experiment in multiracial democracy called Reconstruction, the forces of racism would rise up to subordinate black Americans in the brutal and long regime of Jim Crow. In short, the Union won the most barbaric of nineteenth-century wars, but white supremacy and imperial expansionism won the American peace. By the end of the nineteenth century, conquest and reservations loomed large for indigenous peoples, Mexican lands had been fully annexed, Asian workers had been deported, and the U.S. terrorism of Jim Crow reigned over most black Americans. With the end of continental expansion—Manifest Destiny fulfilling its national mission—transcontinental expansionism flourished.

The Civil War was the first modern war—a use of modern technology and the resources of a modern state for mass mobilization. In this way, the fight over race and empire literally pushed the American democratic experiment into modernity. But that modernity brought temptations and challenges of its own for our democracy. In the wake of the war, triumphant industrialism ran amok, and the dogma of free-market fundamentalism reigned supreme. The country gave birth to a new breed of plutocrats, the "robber barons," who ran unregulated monopolies and accumulated obscene financial fortunes. Ironically, the rights of these corporations were defended in the name of the Fourteenth Amendment enacted to defend the rights of black Americans. The link between transcontinental expansion and plutocratic wealth should not go unnoticed. Empire and corporate elite power, alongside race dividing the citizenry at home, are the age-old formula of nihilistic rule in America.

The American democratic experiment entered the twentieth century as a full-fledged empire with overseas possessions (Hawaii, Cuba, the Philippines, Guam, Puerto Rico, Samoa—or over six million peoples of color) and with domestic racist systems of terror over black, brown, Asian, and red peoples. It also had attained hemispheric hegemony over South and Central America by giving new force and enforcement to the Monroe Doctrine, which in 1823 first stipulated U.S. imperial "sovereignty" over the South American and Central American nations. Most peoples of color were confined to poor rural communities, and wave after wave of immigration from Europe filled U.S. cities with a new population to be exploited as cheap laborers. The formula of corporate elite power alongside racist division of the citizenry would seem to have prevailed; yet, fortunately, this formula often overreaches, resulting in corruption, graft, greed, internal bickering, and a democratic backlash.

The complex intertwining of democratic commitment and nihilistic imperialism is at the heart of our democracy, and democratic commitment has made great strides. There have always been countervailing democratic forces pushing for the realization of the democratic vision expressed in the Declaration. The three most indigenous forms of democratic radicalism initiated by white males in the American democratic experiment—populism, progressivism, and trade unionism—made major contributions to taming the corruption, graft, and greed of plutocratic elites and corrupt politicians. The farmers-led populist movement was a backlash against the free-market fundamentalism of "the money kings" and "the business princes" of the Gilded Age. It called for more democratic participation of rural producers in the shaping of government and business policy. The progressive movement was an urban middle-class backlash against the corrupt ties of politicians to corporate elites and the unfettered greed of financial bosses. It called for more democratic input and bureaucratic efficiency over public policy. The trade-union movement was the worker-led backlash (often by new immigrants) against the free-market fundamentalism of corporate owners and financial bosses. It called for more democratic control over the workplace, especially more say in wages paid to laborers.

These three crucial movements all expressed, in different ways, the democratic aspirations of predominantly white male citizens within the limits of the American empire of that day. Rarely did either movement target white supremacy or imperial expansion. In fact, all three movements tended to be xenophobic and imperialist even as they were deeply democratic. They stand as vital achievements in deepening our democracy, and yet we must acknowledge the limits of each in coming to terms with the legacy of race and empire, as well as the need for continued vigilance on all three of these crucial fronts. The Georgia congressman Thomas Watson, nominated in 1904 and 1908 for president by the Populist Party, was one of the most courageous Populists—often willing to fight alongside black farmers in the Jim Crow South—yet he ended his populist career as a major proponent of the Ku Klux Klan. Woodrow Wilson was an exemplary progressive politician who struggled sincerely against the corporate abuse of power. Yet one of his first acts as president was to reinstate white supremacist segregation throughout the U.S. capital, and his famous freedom charter in foreign policy did not extend to Africa, Asia, or Latin America. Eugene Debs was one of the greatest trade unionists as well as the leader of the U.S. Socialist Party. His crusade against vast wealth inequality was legendary, yet despite his own antiracist views, he could not convince his organization to integrate with peoples of color.

The energetic armies of American democrats won terrific battles against the dogma of free-market fundamentalism, but they fell far short of completing the task of fulfilling the dream of democracy for all peoples. As the American empire reluctantly joined the great world struggles in the twentieth century against the nihilistic forces of imperialism and fascism, it did so with great battles yet to be waged within as well.

The age of Europe—begun in 1492 with the European discovery of the Americas and the expulsion of the Jews and Muslims from Spain—ended in 1945 with the Nazi effort to annihilate all Jews and with the American empire at the center of the world-historical stage. With the advent of the guns of August in 1914, sounding the opening shots of World War I, race and empire were the invisible perimeters of American democracy—hardly seen by most whites yet harshly lived by most peoples of color. The war not only shattered European myths of progress and illusions of security, but also disclosed the brutal realities and bestial desires of imperial Europe. As major European empires collapsed—such as the Austro-Hungarian, Ottoman, and Czarist Russian empires—seismic shifts took place across the globe. The British empire, first shaken by the South Afrikaner anti-imperialist victory at the turn of the century and hobbled by World War I, pulled back financially and militarily in Latin America and Asia. The French, Dutch, and Belgian empires adjusted accordingly. And the humiliated German empire turned inward for later dreams of world domination under the imperial xenophobe Hitler. American imperial banks and corporations quickly filled in for British ones as the world braced for round two in imperial Europe's thirty-year war. As the British pound faltered and the gold standard collapsed, worldwide depression set in.

The aspirations for social and economic advancement among the poor and nonwhite peoples of America were dealt a devastating blow with the onset of the Great Depression. If the business of America is business, as President Calvin Coolidge said, then the America of dreams was no more. In the language of the greatest American play, *The Iceman Cometh*, written in 1939 by the greatest American playwright, the disillusioned democrat Eugene O'Neill, America was a barren landscape of pipe dreams—a landscape littered with the debris of hubris, greed, and bigotry. O'Neill saw no way out—even Socratic questioning and prophetic witness were hopeless. Some looked to the new Soviet empire for inspiration, but its brief alliance with Hitler and Stalinist atrocities dampened their hopes. Needless to say, imperial Europe entered a long, deep tunnel with only the courageous sheer will of imperial Winston Churchill standing between Nazi domination and any democratic possibility in Europe. Fascism—especially the vicious democratic despotism of Hitler (elected by the German people)—cast its ugly shadows over much of imperial Europe, including his fascist allies in Italy (Mussolini) and Spain (Franco). With aggressive militaristic autocrats in Japan seizing Asian lands and with all of Africa under European empires (including the Italian fascists' subjugation of Ethiopia for a short time), only the American and Soviet empires seemed capable of combating the Nazi conquest of the world. And that is precisely what the historical alliance of the American and Soviet empires did together— they defeated the fascist forces on the globe at a cost of fifty million dead, including six million Jews in Nazi concentration camps along with Gypsies, Communists, gays, and lesbians. The indescribable courage of the U.S. Jim Crow armed forces (365,000 dead) and the incredible gallantry of the Soviet army (twenty million Russian dead) gave the world another chance for democracy matters.

A small former British outpost had become the greatest imperial power in the world—with only a devastated Soviet empire as competition. Yet race still haunted the American empire, which was especially ironic given its heroic victory over a racist German regime in Europe. With the mushroom clouds over Hiroshima and Nagasaki to symbolize the defeat of imperial Japanese aims of domination, imperial America was the last behemoth standing after the nihilistic frenzy of a world drunk with power and greed subsided.

Yet, as is often the case in our sad human comedy, the peace did not last long, and in the cold war between the American and Soviet empires that immediately heated up in Turkey, Greece, Germany, and Korea, the major ideological weapon the Soviet empire could use against the democratic claims of the American empire was its racist treatment of black Americans and the refusal of the United States to support freedom movements in colonized Africa, Asia, and poverty-ridden Latin America. Then, as now, race and empire loomed large in America's credibility in arguing about democracy matters on the global stage. No one in his right mind could deny the vicious forms of repression and regimentation in the Soviet empire—as well as Mao's China—yet innocence and denial of race and empire in America vastly weakened a case that could have been stronger if candor had prevailed.

Just as World War II lifted the American economy out of the

Great Depression, the cold war created a military-industrial complex in the United States that produced a vast concentration of military might—unprecedented in human history. Such might tends to intoxicate most, if not all, high-level public officials. To have such power at one's command is itself nearly inhumane, and to remain anchored in one's integrity and humility is nearly impossible. We should not be surprised when we get beneath the empty clichés and routine shibboleths so often uttered by American officials to discover that the obsession with power and might is so prevalent. Only the accountability of an informed citizenry and the intractability of a just rule of law can thwart the nihilism of imperial elites—here or anywhere else.

This difficult lesson of the strength of the forces of nihilism within our democracy was taught most graphically by the black freedom movement led by Martin Luther King Jr. He understood it would take tremendous Socratic questioning, prophetic witness, and tragicomic hope to break the back of American apartheid. Yet he also realized it would take even more vision and courage to dismantle the imperial dimensions of the American democratic experiment and to provide genuine equality of opportunity to all. When he said that bombs dropped on Vietnam also landed in American ghettos—and in white Appalachia, on yellow street corners, in red lands, brown barrios, or black hoods—he was highlighting the close link between empire, class, and race; between imperial wars, wealth inequality, and racist practices. He died because his vision and courage were simply too much for the nihilists to stand—especially the FBI. His life—the intersection of love and democracy—constituted the most powerful threat to the mendacity and hypocrisy of the nihilists drunk with power, driven by greed, or blind to a more democratic future.

King provided Americans with our last great call to conscience about the intertwined evils of race and empire, calling on us to choose between democracy and empire, between democracy and white supremacy, between democracy and corporate plutocracy. (We would add between democracy and patriarchy, homophobia, and ecological abuse.) Since his death, we've witnessed a conservative realignment of the citizenry principally owing to racially coded appeals (crime, busing, welfare, affirmative action). We have seen the southernization of American politics and the de facto racial segregation of American schools, churches, and neighborhoods. King's movement did slay (legal) Jim Crow, yet (actual) Jim Crow Jr. is alive and well. And on the global front, American imperialism rules—with invasions of Grenada, Panama, Nicaragua, Afghanistan, Iraq (though not troubling with U.S.-friendly dictators in Indonesia, Pakistan, Saudi Arabia, or China). The overthrow of Saddam Hussein's ugly totalitarian regime was desirable, yet we supported him for many years and have yet to fulfill any substantive promise of Iraq's democratization. In this way, our imperial invasion fits a pattern of U.S. interests, not democratic principle.

Americans must realize that America truly has become an empire—a military giant, a financial haven, a political and cultural colossus in the world. The U.S. military budget accounts for over 40 percent of the world's total military spending. It is six times the size of the military spending of the number two nation (Russia) and more than that of the next twenty-three nations combined. America is the greatest nuclear power (nine thousand nuclear warheads) and has over 650 military facilities with 1.45 million soldiers in 132 countries (on every continent except Antarctica). And its firepower—missiles, ships, smart bombs, robotic weapons, airplanes, and tanks—is unrivaled in history, past and present. In finance, the U.S. dollar is the global reserve currency—with the stocks on Wall Street constituting two-thirds of the value of the world's stock markets. The United States is the world's biggest debtor nation because foreign investors hold their savings and reserves in dollars for security. American trade and budget deficits as well as American consumer debts are sustained by this foreign investment.

The most powerful international financial institutions—the World Bank, the International Monetary Fund, and the Multilateral Development Banks—are U.S.-dominated. Yet only 0.2 percent of the total gross national product of the United States goes to foreign aid—more than 50 percent of it to Israel and Egypt. The poorest nations, especially in Africa, receive hardly a drop in the bucket. In global politics, the largely U.S.-financed United Nations is disproportionately influenced by U.S. interests—with its symbolic veto power in the Security Council (along with Russia, China, Britain, and France). And the clever deals, outright bribery, or raw bullying of some of the other 190 nations in the world reflect U.S. political prowess. On the cultural front, the seductive presence of McDonald's, Starbucks, Wal-Mart, Coca-Cola, hip-hop, and Hollywood around the world is astounding.

The fundamental question of any serious engagement of

democracy matters in the age of the American empire is how to make the world safe for the legacy of Martin Luther King Jr. and his secular democratic allies of all colors. If we want to do a better job of promoting democracy around the world, solving difficult problems at the heart of the Middle East, and facing the other challenges to democracy that will inevitably present themselves, then we will need to reckon finally with the depth of racism and imperialism we have inflicted not only on so many of our own people but on the peoples of color around the world as well.

To talk about race and empire in America is to talk about how one musters the courage to think, care, and fight for democracy matters in the face of a monumental eclipse of hope, an unprecedented collapse of meaning, and a flagrant disregard for the viewpoints and aspirations of others. Niggerization in America has always been the test case for examining the nihilistic threats in America. Yet we rarely view niggerization as constitutive of America—just as we rarely think nihilism is integral to America. For so long niggerization has been viewed as marginal and optimism central to America. But in our time, when we push race to the margins we imperil all of us, not just peoples of color. If we are to grapple with the contemporary forces of evangelical, paternalistic, and sentimental nihilism prevailing in the country today, we must draw on the deep well of insight into the scars of our racism and imperialism to be found in the democratic tradition that has run alongside those nihilistic forces. The voices and views of nihilistic imperialism may currently dominate our discourse, but they are not the authentic voice of American democracy.

The major shortcoming of our contemporary nihilists—evangelical, paternalistic, and sentimental ones—is that they lack a sub-stantive democratic vision grounded in a deep commitment to the ideals they profess to uphold. Evangelical nihilists like President Bush and Karl Rove give us a raw and robust imperial vision of America as a lone sheriff unilaterally policing a world more and more dependent on foreign oil, trade, and investment while ob-scene wealth inequality escalates at home. In short, to them gen-uine democracy matters little, plutocracy reigns, and empire rules. Paternalistic nihilists such as Senator Hillary Clinton and Senator John Kerry put forward a seductive yet weak technocratic vision of America as the economic engine of a global economy that uses its soft (nonmilitary) power to ensure its hegemony while wealth in-equality stabilizes (or slightly declines) at home. On this view, democracy matters somewhat, corporate elites reign tempered by some liberal conscience, and empire speaks softly and carries a big stick. Namely, the paternalistic nihilists have all too willingly accepted the script put out by the evangelical nihilists of the American empire, so we, as a mass public, have not engaged in the deep questioning that might have followed 9/11. Ironically, the sen-timental nihilists of the media, who ought to have encouraged this questioning, instead all too happily accepted the Bush adminis-tration's script about WMDs and Saddam's links to Al Qaeda, and relished the media frenzy of war, even as they failed to spotlight the truth about Bush's tax cuts or put their lens on the environmental and social travesties being inflicted by the administration. They are becoming mere parasites on their evangelical and paternalis-tic nihilist hosts.

The aim of this book is to put forward a strong democratic vision and critique, rooted in a deep democratic tradition forged on the nightside of the precious American democratic experiment—a tradition of Socratic examination, prophetic practice, and dark hope. This vision takes us far beyond those of the American nihilists. It is a Socratic-driven, prophetic-centered, tragicomic-tempered, blues-inflected, jazz-saturated vision that posits America as a confident yet humble democratic experiment that should shore up international law and multilateral institutions that preclude imperial arrangements and colonial invasions; that should also promote wealth-sharing and wealth-producing activities among rich and poor nations abroad; and that should facilitate the principled transfer of wealth from well-to-do to working and poor people by massive investments in health care, education, and employment, and the preservation of our environment. On this vision—filtered through the lens of race in America—democracy matters much, hardworking and poor citizens reign, and empire is dismantled so that all nations and peoples can breathe freely and aspire to democracy matters, if they have the courage and vision to do so.

3

THE DEEP DEMOCRATIC
TRADITION IN AMERICA

We are a people tending toward democracy at the level of hope;
on another level, the economy of the nation, the empire of
business within the republic, both include in their basic premise the concept of perpetual warfare. . . . But around and under
and above it is another reality; like desert-water kept from the
surface and the seed, like the old desert-answer needing its
channels, the blessing of much work before it arrives to act and
make flower. This history is the history of possibility. . . . All we
can do is believe in the seed, living in that belief.

—Muriel Rukeyser, *The Life of Poetry* (1949)

If the first hope of the democrat is the hope of building in the
zone of overlap between the conditions of practical progress
and of individual emancipation, the second hope is that this
work respond to the felt needs and aspirations of ordinary men
and women. Democracy cannot go forward as the unrecognized
gift of a cunning history to a reluctant nation.

—Roberto Mangabeira Unger,
Democracy Realized: The Progressive Alternative (1998)

To many, our democratic system seems so broken that they have simply lost faith that their participation could really matter. The politics of self-interest and catering to narrow special interests is so dominant that so many ask themselves, Why vote?

This disaffection stems both from the all-too-true reality of the corruptions of our system and from a deeper psychic disillusionment and disappointment. The political discourse is so formulaic, so tailored into poll-driven, focus-group-approved slogans that don't really say anything substantive or strike at the core of our lived experience; the lack of authenticity of discourse—and the underlying lack of gravitas, of penetrating insight and wisdom on the part of politicians—is numbing. But we must keep in mind that the disgust so many feel comes from a deep desire to hear more authentic expressions of insights about our lives and more genuine commitments to improving them. Many of us long for expressions of real concern both about the pain of our individual lives and about the common good—hence the power of Bill Clinton's claim that he felt our pain—as opposed to the blatant catering to base interests and to narrow elite constituencies. We long for a politics that is not about winning a political game but about producing better lives.

The reality of what we get is so far from this that the hope for the kind of authentic voice in our politics that we want to hear has come to seem almost ridiculously naive. And yet, it is the longing for such honest discourse that was surely behind the passion of the early support for Howard Dean. It was no accident that he so energized younger adults in particular—they tend to be less beaten down by the disillusionments of the system. For this reason the angry anti-Bush rhetoric that Dean had to offer was for a while emotionally satisfying, but it was ultimately too limited. It lacked the substance of deeper insights and a positive democratic vision. Both the Republican "vision" and the Democratic "vision" are deeply problematic. Our national focus has become so dominated by narrow us-versus-them discourse that it has all but drowned out authentic debate over issues. Though many voters are mobilized by the increased polarization of our party politics, there is an underlying disgust about the preoccupation of our political leaders with partisan warfare.

The uninspiring nature of our national political culture has only enhanced the seductiveness of the pursuit of pleasure and of diverting entertainments, and too many of us have turned inward to a disconnected, narrowly circumscribed family and social life. White suburbanites and middle-class blacks (and others) are preoccupied with the daily pursuit of the comfort of their material lives. In many cases they literally wall themselves off into comfortable communities, both physical and social, in which they can safely avert their eyes from the ugly realities that afflict so many of our people. Because they are able to buy the cars and take the vacations they want, they are all too willing to either disregard the political and social dysfunctions afflicting the country or accept facile explanations for them.

The black community is increasingly divided, the upper and middle classes as against the feeble institutions of the inner cities. Too much of the black political leadership has become caught up in the mainstream political game and has been turning away from the deep commitment to a more profound advocacy for poor blacks. Meanwhile a generation of blacks who have suffered from the cataclysmic breakdown of the civic and social structure in the inner cities are consigned to lives of extreme alienation and empty pursuit of short-term gratifications.

The emptiness of our political culture has also driven a surge of civically engaged religiosity in the form of the rise of the religious Right, with its misguided righteousness and its narrow, exclusionary, and punitive perspective on the country's social ills. The impulse to join in this massively energized movement may well come from the desire to rise above the emptiness of what strikes its followers as a depraved culture that has lost its moral rudder, but the movement is violating the very ethics of compassion and ecumenicalism that it professes to live by. So zealous has this movement become that it has turned into a hugely divisive and antidemocratic force in the country.

As we take a hard look at our democracy, therefore, the resurgent imperialism of the Bush administration must not set the limits of our critique; repudiating the Bush administration is not enough. Turning back to multilateralism, and to tax and social policies that no longer grossly favor the already well off, are essential missions, but we should take this challenging moment as an opportunity for a deeper soul-searching. Our democracy is suffering from more serious psycho-social ills. This is where what I call the deep democratic tradition becomes so vital.

The dissonance of being both a person who ardently believes in democratic ideals—how can we not fall in love with them if and when we are exposed to them?—and a wide-eyed realist about the dispiriting truths of everyday life in America can be alternately enraging, numbing, and crushing. But that dissonance has also provoked our most impassioned and profound indictments of America's democratic failures, from Ralph Waldo Emerson's championing of the necessity of self-cultivation and his praise of John Brown's radical abolitionism, to Herman Melville's darkly tragic portrayal of Ahab's crazed imperialistic nihilism, to Mark Twain's sly indictment of white supremacy, to James Baldwin's and Toni Morrison's profound explorations of the psychic scars of racism, and to Tupac Shakur's eloquent outrage. The violence-obsessed and greed-driven elements of American culture project themselves out to the world so powerfully—and offensively—that the world has developed a problematic love-hate relationship with America, the ugly extremes of which we are now forced to confront. But legions of Americans have been equally affronted by the perversion of our democratic ideals.

This democratic vigilance has been disproportionately expressed by artists, activists, and intellectuals in American life. They have and can play a unique role in highlighting the possibilities and difficulties of democratic individuality, democratic community, and democratic society in America. They have been the primary agents of our deep democratic tradition. The penetrating visions and inspiring truth telling of Ralph Waldo Emerson, Walt Whitman, Herman Melville, and Eugene O'Neill, of W. E. B. Du Bois, James Baldwin, John Coltrane, Lorraine Hansberry, and Toni Morrison, exemplify the profound potential of democracy in America.

These are the figures whose ferocious moral vision and fervent democratic commitment have held the feet of the plutocratic and

imperial elites to the fire and instilled a sense of purpose to democratic activism on the part of citizens from all colors and classes.
They have been the life force behind the deeper individual and
civic American commitment to democracy.

The deep democratic tradition did not begin in America and we
have no monopoly on its promise. But it is here where the seeds of
democracy have taken deepest root and sprouted most robustly.
The first grand democratic experiment in Athens was driven by a
movement of the demos—citizen-peasants—organizing to make the
Greek oligarchs who were abusing their power accountable.
Democracy is always a movement of an energized public to make
elites responsible—it is at its core and most basic foundation the
taking back of one's powers in the face of the misuse of elite power.
In this sense, democracy is more a verb than a noun—it is more a
dynamic striving and collective movement than a static order or
stationary status quo. Democracy is not just a system of governance,
as we tend to think of it, but a cultural way of being. This is where
the voices of our great democratic truth tellers come in.

The two paradigmatic figures of the deep democratic tradition
in America are Ralph Waldo Emerson and Herman Melville, two
democratically charged giants who set in motion distinctive
streams of this tradition. And the most Emersonian of American
democratic intellectuals is James Baldwin, while the most Melvillean
of our democratic intellectuals is Toni Morrison.

The indisputable godfather of the deep democratic tradition in
America is Emerson, a literary artist of dramatic and visionary elo-
quence and the first full-blown democratic intellectual in the
United States. Emerson was an intellectual who hungered most of

all to communicate to broad publics. He reveled in the burning social issues of his day (the annihilation of Native Americans, slavery), highlighting the need for democratic individuals to be nonconformist, courageous, and true to themselves. He believed that within the limited framework of freedom in our lives, individuals can and must create their own democratic individuality. He understood that democracy is not only about the workings of the political system but more profoundly about individuals being empowered and enlightened (and suspicious of authorities) in order to help create and sustain a genuine democratic community, a type of society that was unprecedented in human history. And he knew that mission required questioning prevailing dogmas as well as our own individual beliefs and biases. A democratic public must continuously create new attitudes, new vocabularies, new outlooks, and new visions—all undergirded by individual commitment to scrutiny and volition. He refused to accept the conventional wisdom of leaders and the narrow pronouncements of experts. In his famous essay "Self-Reliance," he writes:

> Whoso would be a man must be a nonconformist. He who would gather immortal palms must not be hindered by the name of goodness, but must explore if it be goodness. Nothing is at last sacred but the integrity of your own mind.

And also:

> There is a time in every man's education when he arrives at the conviction that envy is ignorance; that im-

itation is suicide; that he must take himself for better for worse as his portion; that though the wide universe is full of good, no kernel of nourishing corn can come to him but through his toil bestowed on that plot of ground which is given to him to till. The power which resides in him is new in nature, and none but he knows what that is which he can do, nor does he know until he has tried.

Emerson offered the empowering insight that to be a democratic individual is to be flexible and fluid, revisionary and reformational in one's dealings with fellow citizens and the world, not adhering to comfortable dogmas or rigid party lines. He posits that the core of being a democrat is to think for one's self, judge for one's self, trust one's self, rely on one's self, and be serene in one's own skin—without being self-indulgent, narcissistic, or self-pitying. This was not a standard beyond the enactment of everyday people, and the concerns of everyday people were the proper focus of democratic inquiry. In "The American Scholar," Emerson declares:

> The literature of the poor, the feelings of the child, the philosophy of the street, the meaning of household life, are the topics of the time. It is a great stride. It is a sign—is it not? of new vigor when the extremities are made active, when currents of warm life run into the hands and the feet. I ask not for the great, the remote, the romantic; what is doing in Italy or Arabia; what is Greek art, or Provencal minstrelsy; I embrace

the common, I explore and sit at the feet of the fa-
miliar, the low.

Emerson's democratic individual is a freedom fighter against
those obstacles that stand in the way of a rich individuality, especially weighty dogma, crusty custom, and suffocating prejudice.
The dominant American ideal of individual upward mobility was
espoused by Herbert Hoover:

> It is by the maintenance of equality of opportunity
> and therefore of a society absolutely fluid in freedom
> of the movement of its human particles that our indi-
> vidualism departs from the individualism of Europe.
> We resent class distinction because there can be no
> rise for the individual through the frozen strata of
> classes and no stratification of class can take place in
> a mass livened by the free rise of its particles.

Yet this is but a portion of Emerson's ideal of deep democratic individuality. He indeed applauds equality of opportunity, but he
criticizes the narrow American dream of material prosperity as a
form of conformism and sleepwalking that overlooks more fundamental goods like character and virtue. He notes:

> Men such as they are, very naturally seek money or
> power; and power because it is as good as money. . . .
> And why not? For they aspire to the highest, and this,
> in their sleep-walking, they dream is highest. Wake

them, and they shall quit the false good and leap to the true. . . . This revolution is to be wrought by the gradual domestication of the idea of Culture. The main enterprise of the world for splendor, for extent, is the upbuilding of a man.

This invasion of nature by trade with its money . . . threatens to upset the balance of man and establish a new Universal Monarchy more tyrannical than Babylon or Rome.

Trade is the lord of the world nowadays—& government only a parachute to this balloon.

There is nothing more important in the culture of man than to resist the dangers of commerce.

Out of doors all seems a market.

In fact, in a low moment, Emerson quipped that "my quarrel with America, of course, was that the geography is sublime, but the men are not." He saw the country as infected with pervasive "selfishness, fraud and conspiracy." He mourned "the American people just as they are, with their vast material interests, materialized intellect and low morals" regulated by a capitalist "system of selfishness . . . of distrust, of concealment, of superior keenness, not of giving but of taking advantage." He darkly concluded that "we are a puny and feeble folk." Yet, though the nightside of America depressed him, he never lost his democratic hope. Although he and America might be "defeated everyday," Americans, he wrote, were "born to victory." This struggle was intensified in his famous efforts to oppose the "removal" of the Cherokee from Georgia in 1835 and to contest the Fugitive Slave Act of 1850. In his public praise of John Brown after the raid on Harpers Ferry and in his celebration of the emancipation of slaves in the West Indies (when he shared the platform with the great Frederick Douglass), Emerson demonstrated a sincere, yet cautious, commitment to activism.

Emerson devoted his life to inspiring the public with his vision of the powers of self-enrichment that our democracy offers and moving them to engage with the issues of the day. He crafted a soaring and emotionally powerful rhetoric that made him the most popular speaker of his time. He believed deeply in the need for democratic intellectuals to exercise powers of persuasion, to take back the public's attention from superficial and unfulfilling diversions, and to hold our public officials to a higher standard. To do just that, he trained his artistic voice to sing in order to spark courage, confidence, and comfort in our perennial struggles to become who we are and what America can be. His inspirations in this regard were the Roman public figures Quintilian and Cicero, who put forth seminal arguments about the powers and the mandates of public rhetoric in terms of keeping a government and society honest and inspiring the public to be engaged.

As the linguist George Lakoff has argued, the imperialist right wing in America today has crafted a conservative rhetoric that has had a seductive effect on the American public, and progressive democrats must come swinging back with a much more persuasive and inspiring rhetoric that speaks to the democratic issues of equality of opportunity, service to the poor, and a focus on public interest.

Emerson took that rhetorical mission seriously, writing prose songs that were meant to unsettle the public, to jolt us out of our sleepwalking and inspire us to stay the democratic course. For Emerson, to be a democratic individual is to speak out on uncomfortable truths; to be an active player in public discourse is to be thrown into life's contingency and fragility with the heavy baggage of history and tradition, baggage like the American legacies of race and empire.

And he put his philosophy of how to be a deep democrat into practice. He left his Unitarian ministry and pastorate because of his disagreement over doctrine. He refused to serve communion due to his iconoclastic beliefs. He then literally became a kind of secular intellectual minister who traveled throughout the country (he gave more than sixty lectures in a year at the age of sixty-two—with no airplanes or air-conditioned hotels!), speaking at lyceums, theaters, forums, or community centers. For over thirty years, Emerson spoke to his fellow citizens in their towns and cities about literature, history, manners, politics, and other sundry topics— face-to-face and soul-to-soul. He was banned from Harvard—his alma mater—for nearly thirty years after his infamous lecture at the divinity school in 1838 that questioned the divinity of Jesus. In that penetrating oration he raised issues that are all too relevant to the crisis of Christianity in America today:

It is time that this ill-suppressed murmur of all thoughtful men against the famine of our churches

. . . should be heard through the sleep of indolence, and over the din of routine. . . .

The stationariness of religion; the assumption that the age of inspiration is past, that the Bible is closed; the fear of degrading the character of Jesus by representing him as a man; indicate with sufficient clearness the falsehood of our theology. It is the office of a true teacher to show us that God is, not was; that He speaketh, not spake. The true Christianity—a faith like Christ's in the infinitude of man,—is lost. . . .

Let me admonish you, first of all, to go alone; to refuse the good models, even those most sacred in the imagination of men, and dare to love God without mediator or veil. . . .

Yourself a newborn bard of the Holy Ghost,—cast behind you all conformity, and acquaint men at first hand with Deity. . . . Look to it first and only . . . that fashion, custom, authority, pleasure, and money are nothing to you,—are not bandages over your eyes, that you cannot see,—but live with the privilege of the immeasurable mind.

Though Emerson's outspoken truth telling generated much elite scorn, the public embraced him. He went on to become the most famous intellectual of his day and the most influential American voice here and abroad. His books, essays, poems, histories, and lectures struck at the heart of democracy matters in nineteenth-century America: his view was that we needed a cultural declaration of independence that required a creative appropriation of the humanist tradition for democratic aims. In "The American Scholar," Emerson prophesies:

> We have listened too long to the courtly muses of Europe. The spirit of the American freeman is already suspected to be timid, imitative, tame. Public and private avarice make the air we breathe thick and fat. . . .
> We will walk on our own feet; we will work with our own hands; we will speak our own minds.

This ebullient proclamation for American self-confidence is couched in a defense of the democratic intellectual—the "Man Thinking"—who recognizes that "the invariable mark of wisdom is to see the miraculous in the common." The great democratic task is to awaken the sleepwalkers in order to take back their powers and take control of their country. In his great essay "Fate," he writes:

> Our America has a bad name for superficialness. Great men, great nations, have not been boasters and buffoons, but perceivers of the terror of life, and have manned themselves to face it.

In his late essay "Intellect," he notes:

> What is the hardest task in the world? To think.

Also particularly relevant to today's situation, Emerson's call for intellectual emancipation in America is neither parochial nor provincial. His democratic sensibility is cosmopolitan and international. He insists on being open to cross-cultural perspectives, on understanding and respecting other traditions from around the world:

> The scholar is that man who must take up into himself all the ability of the time, all the contributions of the past, all the hopes of the future. He must be an university of knowledges.

American self-confidence, he argued, should be grounded not in a narrow chauvinistic claim about the superiority of the American way but rather in a mature affirmation of America's gifts to the world as well as candid acknowledgment of the "most unhandsome part of our condition." Cheap American patriotism not only reflects an immaturity and insecurity, he warned, but also is an adolescent defense mechanism that reveals a fear to engage the world and learn from others. Narrow nationalism is a handmaiden of imperial rule, he argues—it keeps the populace deferential and complacent. Hence it abhors critics and dissenters like Emerson who unsettle and awaken the people. His shining example of democratic intellectual work is a challenge to us today.

This challenge has been taken up through the years by a stream of Emersonian voices—from Walt Whitman to William James, Gertrude Stein, W. E. B. Du Bois, and Muriel Rukeyser. Walt

Whitman became the American bard Emerson called for. From *Leaves of Grass* to *Democratic Vistas*, he expressed a vision of a democratic individuality, community, and society with an unprecedented passion. William James—the great proponent of democratic pragmatism—took philosophy to the street, disparaged America's conflation of gigantism with greatness, and denounced the American imperial aims of his day with passion. Gertrude Stein democratized her sentences in her conversational novels (like *Tender Buttons*) by putting a premium on verbs that dethrone the hierarchy of the conventional grammar and creating an interior monologue for her characters that got beneath superficial banter. W. E. B. Du Bois in *The Souls of Black Folk* lifted the veil over the invisibility of the black individuals, community, and society denied by white supremacist America. And Muriel Rukeyser in her classic *The Life of Poetry* laid bare the democratic aspirations of exploited working people in their creative expressions.

Each of these great Emersonian figures speaks in a democratic idiom of the worth of each individual and the potential of all people to re-create and remake themselves. This Emersonian legacy is a profound effort to keep alive deep democratic energies in the face of rigid ideological dogmas, partisan gamesmanship, and the numbing nihilism of American marketized culture. One can enjoy contemplating what Emerson might have said about the Bush administration's regressive tax cuts and its arrogant unilateralism. And one can imagine how repulsive he would find the us-versus-them rhetoric of the fear-driven vision of our imperial elites.

Penetrating as Emerson's critiques of American politics and life were, the most fully Emersonian of democratic intellectuals in our history was James Baldwin. This is because Baldwin spoke from the position of the oppressed "other" in our culture—as both a black and a gay man—and remade himself out of wretched poverty to become the most wrenching and penetrating critic of the transgressions of imperial and racist America. Like the great Ralph Waldo Ellison—author of the classics *Invisible Man* (1952) and *Shadow and Act* (1964)—Baldwin was a blues-inflected, jazz-saturated democrat. In a heroic fulfillment of Emersonian self-reliance, he emerged from the underside of American civilization—the killing fields and joyful streets of black Harlem U.S.A.—to become America's finest literary essayist of the twentieth century. His artistic eloquence, dramatic insights, and prophetic fire put him at the center of democracy matters for over thirty years. And his powerful and poignant self-examination—always on the brink of despair, yet holding on to a tragicomic hope—bespoke a rare intellectual integrity and personal anguish.

Like Jacob in Genesis 32, Baldwin came out of the midnight struggle a new man with a new name—note his two works, *Nobody Knows My Name* (1961) and *No Name in the Street* (1972)—and a new vision for all of us. This fatherless child—with a loving mother—became the anointed godfather for many democratic activists (like Martin Luther King Jr. and Stokely Carmichael) and artists (like Toni Morrison and Lorraine Hansberry). This black American Socrates was the midwife for new lives, new ideas, and new courage. And he did this the same way Socrates did—by infecting others with the same perplexity he himself felt and grappled with: the perplexity of trying to be a decent human being and thinking person in the face of the pervasive mendacity and hypocrisy of the

American empire. It was his painful commitment to democratic individuality that led him to his art, and he enacted a tough democratic honesty in his art. He wrote in his essay "The Creative Process":

> The artist cannot and must not take anything for granted, but must drive to the heart of every answer and expose the question the answer hides.
>
> We know, in the case of the person, that whoever cannot tell himself the truth about his past is trapped in it, is immobilized in the prison of his undiscovered self. This is also true of nations.

Like Emerson, Baldwin considered his intellectual integrity to be sacred. This led him to be at war—"a lover's war"—with an imperial America that excluded black people from its democratic project. For Baldwin, to be a democratic individual—a self-confident and self-respecting Socratic questioner—in America is to be an "incorrigible disturber of the peace." Unlike Emerson, Baldwin began his quest for democratic individuality as a victim of racist American democracy. Emerson himself noted in his journal on August 25, 1838:

> The whole history of the negro is tragic. By what accursed violation did they first exist that they should suffer always . . . they never go out without being insulted. . . .

Baldwin lived, felt, and breathed this tragic predicament. And even as he wrestled honestly with being niggerized in America, he never lost sight of the democratic potential of America. He saw this potential because he took for granted the humanity of black people—no matter how dehumanized by whites—and always affirmed the humanity of white people—no matter how devilish their treatment of blacks. On that score he wrote in *The Fire Next Time:*

> A vast amount of the energy that goes into what we call the Negro problem is produced by the white man's profound desire not to be judged by those who are not white, not to be seen as he is, and at the same time a vast amount of the white anguish is rooted in the white man's equally profound need to be seen as he is, to be released from the tyranny of his mirror. All of us know, whether or not we are able to admit it, that mirrors can only lie, that death by drowning is all that awaits one there. It is for this reason that love is so desperately sought and so cunningly avoided. Love takes off the masks that we fear we cannot live without and know we cannot live within.

Baldwin spoke the deep truth that democratic individuality demands that white Americans give up their deliberate ignorance and willful blindness about the weight of white supremacy in America. Only then can a genuine democratic community emerge in America—an emergence predicated on listening to the Socratic questioning of black people and the mutual embrace of blacks and whites. Also from *The Fire Next Time*:

> But in order to deal with the untapped and dormant force of the previously subjugated, in order to survive as a human, moving, moral weight in the world, America and all western nations will be forced to re-examine themselves and release themselves from many things that are now taken to be sacred, and to discard nearly all the assumptions that have been used to justify their lives and their anguish and their crimes so long.

For Baldwin, even prior to the criminal acts of white violence and disrespect against black people, "it is the innocence which constitutes the crime." Democratic individuality requires mature and free persons who confront reality, history, and mortality—and who shun innocence, illusion, and purity. In one of the most thought-provoking passages in *The Fire Next Time*, he wrote:

> Perhaps the whole root of our trouble, the human trouble, is that we will sacrifice all the beauty of our lives, will imprison ourselves in totems, taboos, crosses, blood sacrifices, steeples, mosques, races, armies, flags, nations, in order to deny the fact of death. . . . But white Americans do not believe in death, and this is why the darkness of my skin so in-

timidates them and this is why the presence of the Negro in this country can bring about its destruction. It is the responsibility of free men to trust and celebrate what is constant—birth, struggle, and death are constant, and so is love, though we may not always think so—and to apprehend the nature of change, to be able and willing to change. I speak of change not on the surface but in the depths—change in the sense of renewal. But renewal becomes impossible if one supposes things to be constant that are not—safety, for example, or money, or power. One clings then to chimeras, by which one can only be betrayed, and the entire hope—the entire possibility—of freedom disappears. And by destruction I mean precisely the abdication by Americans of any effort really to be free. The Negro can precipitate this abdication because white Americans have never, in all their long history, been able to look on him as a man like themselves. . . .

He [the Negro] is the key figure in his country, and the American future is precisely as bright or as dark as his and the Negro recognizes this, in a negative way. Hence the question: do I really *want* to be integrated into a burning house?

Baldwin knew that a democratic awakening in America will necessarily involve a truer, deeper coalition between the black and white progressive communities. Although the participation of whites in the civil rights movement is often mythologized to be wider and stronger than it was, the fact is that key liberal white groups, such as the mainline prophetic churches and the progressive Jewish community, threw their support behind the movement. Also, the most valuable legislation of Johnson's Great Society program—the Voting Rights Act—would not have passed if Johnson had not been able to count on the coalition of northern white liberals and American blacks.

One of Baldwin's great contributions to American democracy was his determination to delve into the ways in which black thought and culture (especially black music) might instruct and inspire an America caught in a web of self-deception and self-celebration. Black people have wrestled for over three centuries with the harsh dissonance of what America says and thinks about itself versus how it behaves. He believed that by tapping into these black resources, we might be able to create a healthy democratic community and society. In *Many Thousands Gone,* he wrote:

> It is only in his music, which Americans are able to admire because a protective sentimentality limits their understanding of it, that the Negro in America has been able to tell his story. It is a story which otherwise has yet to be told and which no American is prepared to hear. . . .
>
> The story of the Negro is the story of America—or, more precisely, it is the story of Americans. It is not a very pretty story: the story of a people is never very pretty.

Just so, how many white Americans have been drawn into concern for black issues and opened their eyes about racism out of a connection made through respect for and enjoyment of the spirituals, the blues, and jazz, America's most original and grandest art forms? This is a major democratic effect of the great legacy of Mahalia Jackson, John Coltrane, Charlie Parker, Billie Holiday, and Sarah Vaughan.

Baldwin contends that the crisis of the moral decay of the American empire is best met by turning to the democratic determination of black people—looking at America's democratic limits through the lens of race in order to renew and relive deep democratic energies. His point was to highlight their self-confidence, self-trust, tolerance toward others, openness to foreign cultures, willingness to find their own particular voices, and perseverance with grace and dignity in the face of adversity, as well as their solidarity with the downtrodden. The prophetic and poetic voices of hip-hop, like Chuck D or KRS-One, have built on this tradition, speaking more powerfully than any politicians or preachers of our day have been able or willing to do about the hypocrisies of both blacks and whites in American culture.

The murders of Medgar, Malcolm, and Martin were devastating to Baldwin. Vietnam was another wound; the U.S.-supported fascist coup in Chile another bruise; the invisibility of Palestinian suffering in U.S. foreign policy another scar. Even democratic intellectuals can bear only so much. The time was so out of joint—cursed with spite—that he began to wonder whether it could ever be set right. Yet he labored on—comforted more and more by the blues and jazz he cherished and the family he cared so much for. He had made a free artist of himself, had dug as deep as the soul could go, and was as sincere as the Holy Ghost. Yet, he wondered, does America have what it takes to conquer racism and dismantle empire? If so, when will it muster the vision and courage to do so? If not, what are we to do? At his funeral in New York City in 1987, Baldwin himself was heard singing Thomas Dorsey's classic—and Martin Luther King's favorite—song: "Precious Lord, take my hand. Lead me on, let me stand. I am tired, I am weak, I am worn. . . ."

This book is, in part, an extension of the Emersonian tradition in our time. Its vision and analysis is enriched by the powerful Emersonian voices of the past. But there is another stream in the deep democratic tradition from which it also draws, and even more deeply. While the Emersonian tradition emphasizes the vital role of a citizen's individual commitment to democracy and highlights the vast potentials of American democracy, even while nailing its failures to the wall, the special focus of this other tradition is the excoriating critique of America's imperialist and racist impediments to democratic individuality, community, and society. It explicitly makes race and empire the two major limits of the American democratic experiment.

This stream begins in the works of Herman Melville, unappreciated in their time, and still less appreciated than they should be, as damning commentaries on the evils of empire. While the Emersonian is preoccupied with redeeming the soul of America—through its swings from its low to its high moments—the Melvillean tradition seriously questions whether America has a soul, has lost its soul, or ever really had a soul. It begins where Baldwin's disenchantment ends and may leave us with at least one foot (if not both feet) in despair. This stream includes the indispensable Robert Penn Warren, the tragically poetic Eugene O'Neill, the indomitable genius of blues and jazz artists, and the profound fiery witness of Toni Morrison.

Melville's corpus—from *Typee* (1846) to *Billy Budd* (1891)—is an unprecedented and unmatched meditation on the imperialist and racist impediments to democracy in American life. Robert Penn Warren follows Melville's lead and lays bare the depths of white supremacy and imperial realities in the making of America. Such Warren classics as *Brother to Dragons* (1953, 1979—both versions are a scathing critique of Thomas Jefferson's pervasive racism and one-eyed rationalism) and *Chief Joseph of the Nez Percé* (1983; his poem about "the bloody history of the conquest of the West . . . One of the most murderous stories we can think of") are often overlooked and ignored in American letters. Eugene O'Neill's obsession with the nihilism of American imperial and racist rule runs from his first play, *Thirst* (1913), in which he played a mulatto sailor, to his greatest play, *The Iceman Cometh* (1939), which indicts American civilization and the human condition.

Melville is the deep-sea diver of the American democratic tradition; indeed in *Pierre* (1852), he quips:

> Deep, Deep, and still deep and deeper must we go, if we would find out the heart of a man; descending into which is as descending a spiral stair in a shaft, without any end, and where the endlessness is only concealed by the spiralness of the stair and the blackness of the shaft.

Melville's terrifying descent into the unfathomable depths is a plunge not only into existential nothingness but also into the heart of American darkness.

Melville expressed a radical suspicion of the capacity of the American empire to cast aside its childish innocence and confront its nihilistic violence. He grappled with the hard mystery of America's imperial impulse to dominate and conquer others and exposed the martial ideas and monarchical principles hiding behind peaceful language and benign democratic rhetoric. For Melville, beneath the smooth surfaces of American democracy festered the ravages of Amerindian genocide and the damages of African slavery. The self-remaking American individualist—the American gentleman—was also a slaveholder and an Indian annihilator. Again from *Pierre:*

> Pierre's grandfather [was] an American gentleman . . . ; during a fire in the old manorial mansion, with one dash of his foot, he had smitten down an oaken door, to admit the buckets of his negro slaves; . . . in a night-scuffle in the wilderness before the revolutionary war, he had annihilated two Indian savages by making reciprocal bludgeons of their heads. And all this was done by the mildest hearted, and most blue-eyed gentleman in the world . . . the gentlest husband, and the gentlest father; the kindest of masters to his slaves; . . . a sweet-hearted, charitable Christian.

Melville's Ahab in *Moby-Dick* (1851) is a nihilist obsessed with power and might, hell-bent on conquering the axis of evil in his Manichaean (us versus them, good versus evil) vision. Ahab's blind will to conquer the white whale torpedoes his precious ship and crew. His own destruction results from an emptiness and loneliness driven by the dogmatism and nihilism that are metaphorical of an imperial America unable to confront painful truths about itself. As a captain of industry on a floating factory of multiracial workers producing whale oil, Ahab is obsessed with subduing an elusive white whale that simultaneously sustains and maims him. His last words—reminiscent of those of Shakespeare's King Lear and his namesake in 1 Kings 22 in the Old Testament—are: "Oh, lonely death on lonely life! Oh, now I feel my topmost greatness lies in my topmost grief."

Yet Melville's despair about America—or life itself—is not absolute in *Moby-Dick*. His American poetic epic—more than a novel yet not a classical epic poem—begins with the famous line "Call me Ishmael," harkening to the biblical Ishmael, the son of a slave mother. Ishmael is the slim beacon of hope, the only one who survives the journey. And he survives in a coffin-raft given to him by his only friend, Queequeg, a man of color—in stark contrast to the white-dominated ship—whose near death prompted the building of the coffin. Ishmael's survival at the end of the book is therefore due to Queequeg's agency. The carving on the lid of the coffin symbolizes "a mystical treatise on the art of attaining truth." Even as *Moby-Dick* is an indictment of American imperialism, it is also a call for multiracial solidarity.

In fact, Ishmael's journey begins with an encounter with the black underside of America, and his engagement with the vision of America's dark side will push him from innocence to maturity. He begins his story in a state of despair; a despair he longs to overcome by getting "to sea as soon as I can." Waiting for the ship to embark, he goes from inn to inn searching for a place to stay in New Bedford. In searching for the cheapest inn, he finds himself in the black section of town—among those caught in the hellish death grip of imperial and racist America. Melville writes:

> It seemed the great Black parliament sitting in Tophet. A hundred black faces turned round in their rows to peer; and beyond, a black Angel of Doom was beating a book in a pulpit. It was a negro church; and the preacher's text was about the blackness of darkness, and the weeping and wailing and teeth-gnashing there. Ha, Ishmael, muttered I, backing out, wretched entertainment at the sign of "The Trap!"

This black inferno in which the struggle with nihilism is surmounted will mirror his subsequent journey in which the imperial Ahab's wrestling with nihilism leads to devastation. Ellison's invisible man one hundred years later repeats this scene with the preacher speaking on "the blackness of blackness"—another initiation into imperial America through the lens of race. Both Ishmael and the invisible man are exemplary seekers of democratic individuality, community, and society through the black brook of fire in America.

For Melville, this black inferno was not only the vantage point of viewing the American democratic experiment but also the litmus test for assessing the deep democratic tradition in America. The enslavement of Africans and Manifest Destiny over Amerindians proved the noble lie of American democracy. And he felt this on the most intimate of levels. His father-in-law, Lemuel Shaw, was the chief justice of the Supreme Judicial Court of Massachusetts who handed down the most famous test of the Fugitive Slave Law. Shaw ordered the black ex-slave Thomas Sims back to his southern owner. Later, in another infamous case, Shaw decreed that the fugitive ex-slave Anthony Burns return to his owner. Melville's abolitionist sentiments cut against the grain of many in his personal family and national community, but he expressed them nonetheless. Today his loving yet harsh indictment of America rings louder and truer than ever. And he has always resonated with the most acute truth tellers of America. The commitment to self-worth and individual potential of the Emersonian combines with the commitment to deep-searching truth telling of the Melvillean in the most American of art forms, the blues and jazz.

Louis Armstrong and Bessie Smith, Duke Ellington and Ma Rainey, John Coltrane and Sarah Vaughan—all foundational figures of the blues and jazz heritage—created and enacted a profound democratic *paideia*—a cultivation of critical citizenry—in the midst of the darkness of America. If the blues is the struggle against pain for transcendence, then, as Duke Ellington proclaimed, "jazz is freedom." Like Emerson, these great blues and jazz musicians are eloquent connoisseurs of individuality in their improvisational arts and experimental lives. Unlike Emerson, they sit on the edge of America's abyss—in the invisible chocolate infernos of the American paradise. Like Melville, they engage in deep-sea diving beneath the apparent American sunshine. Unlike Melville, they emerge with a strong blood-soaked hope and a seductive tear stained smile. They are the consummate American practitioners of the tragicomic.

This world-historical black confrontation with the absurd in America and the absurd as America—with the frightening American threat to black sanity and dignity in slavery, Jim Crow, and discrimination—produced a distinctive deepening of the democratic tradition in America. This deepening is not simply a matter of the expansion of rights and liberties for all Americans as seen in the social movements led by Frederick Douglass, A. Philip Randolph, Martin Luther King Jr., and Ella Baker. It also has to do with the very meaning of democracy in America—the recasting of the contours of democratic vision and the re-creating of the contents of democratic modes of existence. The blues and jazz made it possible to engage race in America on personal and intimate terms—with democratic results. The great white literary bluesman Tennessee Williams prophetically entitled his first collection of plays *American Blues.* The rich blues and jazz heritage was eventually embraced by white citizens and was especially appealing to the antiestablishment youth behind the infectious pulses of rock. This heritage was the first major cultural point of contact between whites and blacks, and we've seen this dynamic again in the embrace of rhythm and blues and hip-hop by white citizens.

As infectious and embracing as the blues is, we should never forget that the blues was born out of the crucible of slavery and its vicious legacy, that it expresses the determination of a people to assert their human value. The blues professes to the deep psychic and material pains inflicted on black people within the sphere of a mythological American land of opportunity. The central role of the human voice in this heritage reflects the commitment to the value of the individual and of speaking up about ugly truths; it asserts the necessity of robust dialogue—of people needing to listen up— in the face of entrenched dogma. The patient resilience expressed in the blues flows from the sustained resistance to ugly forms of racist domination, and from the forging of inextinguishable hope in the contexts of American social death and soul murder. The blues produced a mature spiritual and communal strength. The stress the blues placed on dialogue, resistance, and hope is the very lifeblood for a vital democratic citizenry.

The most sophisticated exploration of this black enactment of dialogue, resistance, and hope is found in the magisterial corpus of Toni Morrison. The blues and jazz heritage speaks most profoundly and profusely in her literary works. She is the towering democratic artist and intellectual of our time. Morrison's texts embody and enact forms of deep democratic energies unparalleled in America's long struggle with the dark side of its democracy.

She highlights the strong will and potential promise of democratic individuals. Ordinary people taking back their power sit at the center of her artistic vision. Regarding one of her masterpieces, *Beloved* (1987), she states:

> The slaveholders have won if this experience is beyond my imagination and my powers. It's like humor:

you have to take the authority back; you realign where the power is. So I wanted to *take* the power. They were very inventive and imaginative with cruelty, so I have to take it back—in a way that I can tell it.

This profoundly democratic action, of taking back power over one's life—enacted both by Morrison as artist and her characters in her art—is indebted to Emersonian nonconformity and resistance to prevailing authority. But like Melville, Morrison is also keenly alert to the formidable impediments to democratic individuality and community. One of her most vivid characters, Sethe in *Beloved*, explains why she killed her daughter, named Beloved, when a fugitive-slave hunter came to take them all back to their southern slave owners. Sethe says:

That anybody white could take your whole self for anything that came to mind. Not just work, kill, or maim you, but dirty you. Dirty you so bad you couldn't like yourself anymore. Dirty you so bad you forgot who you were and couldn't think it up. And though she and others lived through and got over it, she could never let it happen to her own. The best thing she was, was her children. Whites might dirty *her* all right, but not her best thing, her beautiful, magical best thing—the part of her that was clean. No undreamable dreams about whether the headless, feetless torso hanging in the tree with a sign on it was her husband or Paul A; whether the bubbling-hot girls in the colored-school fire set by patriots included her daughter; whether a gang of whites invaded her daughter's private parts, soiled her daughter's thighs and threw her daughter out of the wagon. *She* might have to work the slaughterhouse yard, but not her daughter.

And no one, nobody on this earth, would list her daughter's characteristics on the animal side of the paper. No. Oh no.

Morrison's exploration of the heart of American darkness is most essentially a search for the possibility of democratic community—a vision of everyday people renouncing narrow self-interest and creating a web of caring under harsh American circumstances. Morrison notes:

Those people could not live without value. They had prices, but no value in the white world, so they made their own, and they decided what was valuable. It was usually eleemosynary [charitable], usually something they were doing for somebody else. Nobody in the novel, no adult black person, survives by self-regard, narcissism, selfishness. They took the sense of community for granted. It never occurred to them they could live outside of it.

Morrison's debt to Melville is quite conscious and deliberate. He was the first American literary artist to explore whiteness as an ideology and its traumatic effects on blacks and whites. As she writes in her pioneering literary critical text *Playing in the Dark* (1992):

And if the white whale is the ideology of race, what
Ahab has lost to it is personal dismemberment and
family and society and his own place as a human in
the world. The trauma of racism is, for the racist and
the victim, the severe fragmentation of the self and
has always seemed to me a cause (not a symptom) of
psychosis.

In Morrison's vision, it is fear and insecurity that drive the dog-
matisms and nihilisms of imperial elites like Ahab, and love and
hope that bind democratic communities in response to the offenses
of imperial power and might. Melville's artistic integrity and democratic courage left him "very alone, very desperate and very
doomed" in mid-nineteenth-century America. As Morrison com-
ments about Melville's effort:

To question the very notion of white progress, the very
idea of racial superiority, of whiteness as privileged
place in the evolutionary ladder of humankind, and to
meditate on the fraudulent, self-destroying philosophy of that superiority, to "pluck it out from under
the robes of Senators and Judges," to drag the "judge
himself to the bar"—that was dangerous, solitary, radical work. Especially then. Especially now.

But rather than encouraging either revenge or despair,
Morrison, like Baldwin, puts forth a vision of black democratic
identity rooted in a love that embraces all—a love and trust that

holds together a democratic community and society. When asked what is her favorite metaphor for her work, she replied:

> Love. We have to embrace ourselves. . . . James Baldwin once said, "You've already been bought and paid for. Your ancestors already gave it up for you. You don't have to do that anymore. Now you can love yourself." . . .
>
> That's why we're here. We have to do something nurturing that we respect, before we go. We must. It is more interesting, more complicated, more intel-lectually demanding and more morally demanding to love somebody. To take care of somebody. . . .
>
> What is interesting to me is that under the cir-cumstances in which the people in my books live there is this press toward love.

Morrison's powerful portraits of community—also enhanced by her Catholicism—speak to the need for citizens in a democracy to be socially engaged, to involve ourselves with one another's lives. Her message of democratic love resists the narrow arrogance and self-interest of the nihilism taking hold of our society. The most free and democratic character in Morrison's eight powerful nov-els—Pilate in *Song of Solomon* (1978)—says on her deathbed, "I wish I'd a knowed more people. I would have loved 'em all. If I'd a knowed more, I would a loved more." In a commentary on Pilate, Morrison clearly displays her Baldwinian ethic of love and her democratic faith:

That's a totally generous free woman. She's fearless. She's not afraid of anything. She has very few material things. She has a little self-supporting skill that she performs. She doesn't run anybody's life. She's available for almost infinite love. If you need her— she'll deliver. And she has complete clarity about who she is.

For Morrison, this belief in the capacity of everyday people to forge personal dignity and in the power of democratic community to resist the abuse of elite power is the core of America's deep democratic tradition. Like Baldwin, she sees this belief most readily manifest in the black musical tradition. The dangerous freedom embedded in the performance of musical artists is a form of taking back one's powers in the face of one's apparent powerlessness. Morrison notes:

My notion of love . . . is very closely related to blues. There's always somebody leaving somebody, and there's never any vengeance, any bitterness. . . . It's quite contrary to the overwhelming notion of love that's the business of the majority culture.

She is our premier literary musician, and her texts are communal experiences in which the audience participates in and with her performance.

Morrison's aim is to spark in the reader a desire to explore the rich human depths of a dehumanized people, to revel in the forms of linguistic delicacies alongside their social miseries, and to be unsettled by the hypocrisy of an American chamber of horrors as the empire trumpets liberty and opportunity for all. That is why she places so much stress on the cadences of the human voice in her works. As in the blues, this emphasis asserts the dignity and individuality of her characters; it allows us to see inside them and demands that we listen to them. To hear the nuances of voice is to gain some access to the humanity of individuals. To listen closely to the tones of voice is to be open to the interiority of persons. Her democratic mission is to heal—yet to shatter moral numbness and awaken sleepwalking hurts. As she writes: "Anything dead coming back to life hurts." As Ellison wrote, the purpose is to "keep the painful details and episodes of a brutal experience alive in one's aching consciousness" in order to be able to transcend that pain. She enacts on the page what black blues singers perform on the stage—with similar strategies of repetitive refrains, rhythmic language, syncopated sounds, and dark laughter. She writes about her intent:

> My efforts to make aural literature—A-U-R-A-L—work because I do hear it . . . it has to *sound* and if it doesn't *sound* right . . .

> So I do a lot of revision when I write in order to clean away the parts of the book that can *only* work as print. It has to have certain kinds of fundamental characteristics (one of) which is the participation of the *other*, that is, the audience, the reader, and that you can do with a spoken story.

Morrison's subtle grounding in black musical forms poses a serious challenge to her readers. Her books require readers to take part in them. Even a critic as sophisticated and astute as Harold Bloom—usually supremely confident in his literary critiques—openly ponders: "I do not believe that Morrison writes fiction of a kind I am not yet competent to read and judge. . . ."

Morrison's books can also be almost too painful to bear. She transfigures the blues cry in the dark depths with "circles and circles of sorrow." But, as with blues artists, she tells us: "If you surrendered to the air, you could *ride* it." And despite their difficulty, her books have become bestsellers, read avidly by blacks, whites, and others, which is a great testament to the democratic potential residing within the American public.

Morrison's fundamental democratic insight is that there can be democratic dialogue only when one is open to the humanity of individuals and to the interiority of their personalities. Like the blues, Morrison assumes the full-fledged humanity of black people—a revolutionary gesture in a racist civilization—and thereby dethrones the superior status of whites. This assumption liberates both blacks and whites and enables them to embark on a candid, though painful, engagement with life and death, joy and sorrow, resistance and domination, hope and despair in the American empire. Like her beloved Faulkner, Morrison takes us into the underworld and underground of the American Disney World to lay bare the lives of those ambushed by disillusionment and hampered by disappointment.

Morrison is a democratic subversive because she shuns all

forms of authority that suppress the flowering of unique individuality. She heralds all kinds of free self-creations that take seriously quests for wisdom and justice. Her insistence on the need to appreciate the plights and values of all people is a vital guide as we attempt to instill democracy in the Middle East, a region riven by issues of offended identity.

Our democracy is certainly in horrible disrepair, and the disengagement of so many, along with the flight into superficial forms of entertainment and life satisfaction, is understandable. But the deep love of and commitment to democracy expressed by these great artists and the long tradition of scrutinizing the ravages of our imperialism are strong.

The anger and disillusionment that so many Americans have felt toward the Bush administration, especially in regard to the dishonest manipulation in launching the Iraq war, is not a narrowly partisan affair. It is not a matter of the typical polarization of party politics. The passion evoked by the administration comes out of deep commitment to democratic ideals. If the administration had not been betraying those ideals, it would not have had to lie to the public in order to generate support for the war. The impassioned critique on the part of so many Americans of the current American militarism is a testament to just how alive and intense the public commitment to democracy is.

Though the saturation of American market-driven culture around the world has obscured the deep democratic strain in American life, it is in fact in America where democratic intellectuals have had the deepest tradition and greatest impact. The most profound democratic artist and intellectual—Anton Chekhov—did not live in a democratic experiment. We can be inspired by his democratic genius—as seen in his massive popularity in our time—but our American context does not require that we try to get a democratic experiment off the ground (as he did); rather, we must sustain and refine ours before it falls to the ground.

Since American civilization is first and foremost a business culture—a market-driven society—its elected officials and corporate elites are preoccupied with economic growth and national prosperity. That is why it has been primarily artistic, activist, and intellectual voices from outside the political and economic establishments who have offered the most penetrating insights and energizing visions and have pushed the development of the American democratic project.

That deep tradition of democratic artists, activists, and intellectuals is very much alive and well. We have great playwrights like Tony Kushner, August Wilson, and Arthur Miller who never lose sight of democratic individuality as they probe the underside of American life; grand novelists such as Thomas Pynchon, Russell Banks, and of course Toni Morrison who disclose the workings of struggling democratic communities in the face of elite power; major filmmakers like Charles Burnett and the Wachowski brothers who give us a glimpse of crisis-ridden democratic societies in the wake of our information age; and towering social critics like Noam Chomsky and Susan Sontag who wed the humanist tradition to democratic ideals. When Marian Wright Edelman fights to eliminate child poverty, William Greider calls for pension funds to be used to support socially responsible enterprises, Angela Davis questions the role of prisons, Barbara Ehrenreich highlights the plight of the working poor, Dolores Huerta promotes unionization of immigrant workers, or Ralph Nader fights for democratic accountability of corporations, we know the imperialist strain in American life can be resisted. Most important, when visionary and courageous citizens see through the dogmas and nihilisms of those who rule us and join together to pursue democratic individuality, progress can be made in our communities and our society. The deep democratic tradition in America that these and so many other of our most challenging and prophetic artists have called forth and kept alive is the greatest gift of America to the world.

The moral outrage provoked by the arrogant militaristic policies, pro-rich tax cuts, and authoritarian excesses of the Bush administration arise out of this deep well of democratic commitment and are a hopeful sign that a democratizing resurgence may be under way. And it is neither naive nor quixotic to talk about a democratic awakening in the face of the corruption shot through our political and economic system. Our history shows that stirring the deep commitment to democratic values and mandates does make a difference. But we must not confuse this democratic commitment with flag-waving patriotism. The former is guided by common virtues forged by ordinary citizens, the latter by martial ideals promoted by powerful elites. Democratic commitment confronts American hypocrisy and mendacity in the name of public interest; flag-waving patriotism promotes American innocence and purity in the name of national glory.

As we embark on a bold and questionable endeavor to implant democracy in the Middle East, the vital perspectives and admonitions about the painful limits and sometimes brutal arrogance of our own American democracy offered by these profound democratic voices—themselves inspired by and in rich communion with the prophetic voices of the American democratic tradition—must guide us to strive to appreciate the cultural and political complexities of the societies we are so brazenly trying to reshape. The profound insights into the ways in which American democracy has itself condoned disenfranchising practices and created space for brutal suppression of the democratic rights not only of blacks but of Native Americans, Asian and Latino laborers, and European immigrants, and the painful insights into the devastating long-term material and psychic effects of that treatment, must inform our approach to the goal of spreading democracy around the globe. We will likely stoke more resentment in the Middle East than fires of democratic passion if we are not sensitive to the special characteristics out of which democracy must evolve there.

We should not be seduced by the simplistic and self-serving statements from the Bush administration about the commitment to instill democracy in Afghanistan and Iraq—with grand references to spreading democracy throughout the rest of the Middle East—as though democracy is something that can be so easily imposed from the outside, not the least by an arrogant superpower with dubious motives. That is not the true voice of the American democratic tradition; that is the voice of the American imperial tradition. But just as there are powerful voices for democratic progress in the American tradition, both past and present, so there are powerful voices of wisdom and dissent within the Middle East. The need for democratic identities in the Jewish and Islamic worlds looms large, and one of the most urgent questions for democrats in America who oppose the arrogant militarism of the Bush administration is, how can we take back our country so that the deep democratic tradition in America can help forge these democratic identities abroad and be a force for peace and justice in that troubled part of the world?

4

FORGING NEW JEWISH AND ISLAMIC DEMOCRATIC IDENTITIES

Among the peoples of the world, we [the Jews] were the only ones who separated what lived within us from all community with what is dead. For while the earth nourishes, it also binds. Whenever a people loves the soil of its native land more than its own life, it is in danger. . . . The earth betrays a people that entrusted its permanence to earth.

—FRANZ ROSENZWEIG, *The Star of Redemption* (1921)

The American Jew, if I may say so—and I say so with love, whether or not you believe me—makes the error of believing that his Holocaust ends in the New World, where mine begins. My diaspora continues, the end is not in sight, and I certainly cannot depend on the morality of this panic-stricken consumer society to bring me out of—: Egypt.

—JAMES BALDWIN, *The Price of the Ticket* (1985)

If we come to realize that, as many scholars have recently noted, Islamic doctrine can be seen as justifying capitalism as well as socialism, militancy as well as fatalism, ecumenism as well as ex-

clusivism, we begin to sense the tremendous lag between academic descriptions of Islam (that are inevitably caricatured in
the media) and the particular realities to be found within the
Islamic world. . . . But underlying every interpretation of other
cultures—especially of Islam—is the choice facing the individual scholar or intellectual whether to put intellect at the service of power or at the service of criticism, community and
moral sense.

—EDWARD SAID, *Covering Islam* (1981)

The good society is one that is based on three equalities: economic equality, today known as socialism, or the sharing of
wealth; political equality or democracy, or sharing in political
decisions which affect daily life; and social equality which, to
some extent, results from socialism and democracy, and is
characterized by a lack of social classes and discrimination
based on color, faith, race or sex. In the good society, people are
judged according to their intellectual and moral character, as
reflected in their public and private lives and demonstrated in
the spirit of public service at all times and through every means.
Social equality aims at removing social classes and differences
between urban and rural life by providing equal opportunity
for cultural refinement.

—MAHMOUD MOHAMED TAHA,
The Second Message of Islam (1987)

The bloody conflict in the Middle East is too often viewed in
terms of an interminable clash between the Israelis and
the Palestinians or Israel and the Arab world. Rarely do we acknowledge the role of imperialism run amok in having set the conflict in motion. The roots of the conflict go back to the shadows

cast by the British empire, the cold war struggle between the Soviet empire and the American empire, and now the central presence of American imperial support for the Israeli state as well as the Egyptian and Jordanian states. In fact, the very term "Middle East" was coined in 1902 by a leading American imperialist, the U.S. naval officer Alfred Thayer Mahan, to name the geographical space between India and the Arab provinces of the Ottoman empire in an article he wrote about the interests of the Great Powers in the region. In the past, terms such as "Western Asia" or "Turkish Asia" had been used. With the collapse of the Ottoman empire after World War I and the popularizing of the term "Middle East" by the *London Times*, it caught on, and we seem now to be stuck with it.

The popular understanding of the conflict, especially in the United States, has been grossly simplified, and it is rarely viewed through the democratic lens that brings the dire plight of ordinary Israelis and Arabs, Kurds and Turks, Iranians and Iraqis into focus. The very terms of the debate have been disproportionately shaped by the most zealously driven power players, be they in the U.S. government, Islamic states, or Israel. These elites engage in a willful disregard for uncomfortable facts, both historic and current, as well as outright distortions of crucial subtleties of the arguments made by their foes. If there ever was a place and time for the unleashing of deep democratic energies in the region, it is now.

We must begin with the primary concern of all elites in the region—the quest for access to oil. The conflict cannot be understood without acknowledging this fundamental fact. And the crisis cannot be solved without keeping track of the effects of the elites' power plays to secure oil. These effects hamper efforts to put forward deep democratic identities in both Israel and the Islamic countries. Yet there are gallant voices in Jewish communities in America and Israel and in the Islamic world that call for just such democratic identities and practices, and they have yet to be heard with the force they deserve. Democracy matters require that we hear these courageous voices and help them to become more prominent here and on their home turfs.

The legacy of the imperialist quest to secure access to oil in the region is threefold. First and foremost, as the Achilles' heel of U.S. foreign policy in the region, the need to procure oil drives a shameful disregard of the radically undemocratic character of oil-rich autocratic Arab regimes, which remain hostile to Israel's very existence. Second, the ugly thirty-seven-year Israeli occupation of Palestinian lands and subjugation of Palestinian peoples violate international law and any code of humanitarian ethics. The linchpin to any resolution in the region is an end to this unjust and ineffective occupation. Third, the wholesale guarantee of Israeli security against barbaric Palestinian suicide bombers that murder innocent Israeli civilians is necessary. These three fundamental challenges—lack of democracy and presence of anti-Semitic bigotry in oil-rich Arab states, justice for Palestinians, and security for Israel—rest upon promoting deep democratic identities in the region.

This cannot be done with the prevailing American attitudes and policies in the region. For example, in the deeply flawed planning for the postwar period in Iraq, the Bush administration has revealed an appalling lack of either understanding of or concern for the internal situation in the country. The administration has also shown an irresponsible lack of commitment to the regime it set up in Afghanistan. A more genuine approach to inspiring and nur-turing democracy in the region will require the United States to resolve deeply hypocritical contradictions in our dealings with Middle Eastern regimes. We tend to prop up some tyrants while deciding to take out others unilaterally. We look the other way about hypocrisies in Israel's dealings with the Palestinians, and display an inexcusable lack of understanding of Palestinian views in our ef-forts to design a peace plan. We helped install and sustain Saddam Hussein himself, and before him the tyrannical shah in Iran. These unprincipled U.S. power plays backfired when they produced not only regimes hardened against us but also a more general anti-American sentiment in the Middle East. Because of our undeniably crucial role in the region, efforts to forge more authentic democ-racies and to resolve the Israeli-Palestinian conflict must start with the U.S. government and public developing more enlightened views of the complexities of public opinion versus elite power play-ers' positions in the region. At the moment both Israel and the Arab world are currently under the thrall of extremist thinkers and power players. Hence, instead of making deals with these myopic elites, the United States must respect and encourage the demo-cratic voices being stifled in both worlds.

Just as the arrogant, unilateralist views of the Bush adminis-tration have marginalized the deep democratic voices in America in the view of the rest of the world, so have the corrupted and ex-tremist elites in the Arab world and in Israel thwarted the demo-cratic energies within those societies. But democratic energies are there, and we must learn to appreciate and support them in help-ing to forge new democratic identities in the region. These identities must not only cut through all forms of tribalism and parochialism but also cast a limelight on everyday Israelis and Arabs who shun bigotry, desire peace, and yearn to be more than pawns in the power games of Israeli, Arab, and American elites. This goal may seem quixotic because the polarized situation in the Middle East, especially the Israeli-Palestinian conflict, is so intransigent and may even seem intractable. Surely, loosening the constraints to peace will require a herculean effort, but enlightened U.S. policy conjoined with the energy of democratic social movements committed to peace and justice must be stirred. Within Israel and the Arab world, there are strong traditions to spur this change of the prevailing consciousness.

Let us begin with the long and rich prophetic tradition among Jews, past and present. There has been a long struggle within the Jewish community, both in the American Jewish community and in Israel, about the moral hypocrisies of Israel's treatment of the Palestinians, with progressive Jews arguing that the Jewish prophetic tradition requires a more robustly compassionate and democratically just approach. As Rabbi Michael Lerner of *Tikkun* magazine writes in his powerful book *Healing Israel/Palestine* (2003):

> Jews did not return to their ancient homeland to oppress the Palestinian people, and Palestinians did not resist the creation of a Jewish state out of hatred of the Jews. In the long history of propaganda battles between Zionists and Palestinians, each side has at times told the story to make it seem as if the other side was consistently doing bad things for bad rea-

sons. In fact, both sides have made and continue to make terrible mistakes. . . . As long as each side clings to its own story, and is unable to acknowledge what is plausible in the story of the other side, peace will remain a distant hope.

Those of us who are both pro-Israel and pro-Palestine, who truly believe in the validity of the state of Israel and truly believe in the decency of the vast majority of the Palestinian people, and who will not accept the crude distortions that go for analysis in American media and politics (e.g., that the Palestinians were offered a great deal by Barak, or that the Palestinian people will settle for nothing less than the full destruction of Israel), are systematically excluded when the media represents the sides of the conflict.

The barbarity of the terrorism launched against Jews in Israel first by the Arab states and now by the suicide bombers is real and should never be explained away—as the zealots on the Palestinian side do—but the dominant Jewish stance has become so hardened by the pain of this suffering, and by the feeling of being so reviled by enemies, that the Jewish community has been losing touch with its own rich prophetic tradition.

We recall that the Jewish invention of the prophetic, to be found in the scriptural teachings of Amos, Hosea, Isaiah, Micah, Jeremiah, and Habakkuk, not only put justice at the center of what it means to be chosen as a Jewish people but also made compassion to human suffering and kindness to the stranger the fundamental features of the most noble human calling. The divine covenant with Abraham, the divine deliverance of enslaved Jews from Egypt, the divine pathos against injustice in Amos, and the divine promise of salvation in Isaiah all speak to the core of the prophetic: the distinctive Jewish refusal to allow raw power to silence justice or might to trump right. At the heart of the prophetic in the Hebrew scripture is an indictment of those who worship the idol of human power. According to the scripture, since human beings cannot be divine—and often act quite devilishly—prophetic voices must remind Israel of what God requires of them: "To do justice, to love kindness and to walk humbly with your God" (Micah 6:8). The very covenant—not contract—between God and Israel is predicated on God's love for justice and Israel's charge: "To keep the way of the Lord by doing righteousness and justice" (Genesis 18:19). The prophetic figures in Israelite history—Jeremiah, Micah, Amos, Isaiah, and others—give voice to *divine* compassion and justice in order to awaken *human* compassion and justice.

Prophetic witness consists of human deeds of justice and kindness that attend to the unjust sources of human hurt and misery. It calls attention to the causes of unjustified suffering and unnecessary social misery and highlights personal and institutional evil, including the evil of being indifferent to personal and institutional evil. The especial aim of prophetic utterance is to shatter deliberate ignorance and willful blindness to the suffering of others and to expose the clever forms of evasion and escape we devise in order to hide and conceal injustice. The prophetic goal is to stir up in us the courage to care and empower us to change our lives and our historical circumstances.

The Jewish prophetic tradition is central to democracy matters because the perennial question for any democracy, especially for imperial nations, is always, how is the public interest informed and influenced by the most vulnerable in our society? The Jewish invention of the prophetic put a premium on this query in an un-precedented manner. Rabbi Michael Lerner, following his teacher, the great Abraham Joshua Heschel, is representative of this Judaic prophetic tradition.

How sad it is to move from this grand Judaic insight of the prophetic to the bloodshed and bigotry, myopia and idolatry of the Israeli-Palestinian conflict. Both peoples are currently led by such arrogant and stubborn leaders—Sharon and Arafat—locked to-gether in escalating and reinforcing spirals of violence. Both lead principally because of their manipulation of the deep fear and paranoia of their respective peoples—and an understandable fear and paranoia it is. But that paranoia has been used by the nihilis-tic xenophobes on both sides. On the Jewish side are zealous colo-nial settlers who envision a greater Israel that entails a full-blown apartheid condition for Palestinians, and on the Palestinian side are suicide bombers who call for Jewish annihilation. It is clear that this seemingly intractable impasse cannot be settled by the Israelis and Palestinians acting alone. Sharon's government re-fuses to substantially dismantle Israel's imperial settlements or give up colonial occupation. Arafat's government refuses to stop the barbaric suicide bombers or punish in any consequential way those who work to push the Jews into the sea. Anti-Arab racism and anti-Jewish racism delimit the democratic possibilities among both peoples. The only hope for a peace with justice is either for the autocratic Arab states to intervene by ensuring Israeli security and accepting Israeli legitimacy or for the American empire to wed its indispensable diplomatic and financial support to democratic and anti-imperial ends.

The major obstacle to peace in the region is the autocratic rule of Arab elites and their support, whether explicit or implicit, of anti-Jewish terrorism—the heinous terrorism of suicide bombers has dealt a devastating blow to peace—but the special relationship between the United States and Israel and Israeli violence against the Palestinians have also played crucial roles in the deepening of the conflict.

There is no doubt that the relationship of the American empire and the Israeli state is a special one. It was not always so. Nor will it likely forever be so. Most American political elites supported the Arab states in the late 1940s and early 1950s owing to oil. In 1956 President Eisenhower ordered Israel to withdraw from the Gaza Strip and Sinai Peninsula, which it had invaded and occupied, along with oil-hungry Britain and Nasser-hating France. Israel complied. The present U.S.-Israeli alliance did not emerge until the mid-1960s. Soviet ties to Egypt and Syria pushed President Johnson closer to Israel. Meanwhile, Israel's fear of Arab threats to eliminate the Jewish state made it eager for U.S. support. The first U.S. offensive weapons systems sale to Israel—the A4 Skyhawk jet deal—was approved in 1965.

When, in 1967, Egypt's Nasser closed the Strait of Tiran, the waterway that gave access to Israel's only port on the Red Sea, Israel launched its historic preemptive attack on Egypt and Syria—an attack that was approved by the CIA and the Pentagon during the visit of Meir Amit (Israel's chief of Mossad) on the eve of the action—which led to the Six Days' War. The next fall the United States sold Phantom jets to Israel, making this weapon available for the first time to an ally outside of NATO, even before giving it to South Vietnamese forces who were fighting a war in which U.S. soldiers were dying daily. U.S. military sales to Israel were $140 million between 1968 and 1970. This jumped to $1.2 billion from 1971 to 1973. After the Israeli defeat of the Soviet client states of Egypt and Syria in the 1973 Yom Kippur War, U.S. military aid increased still further. In 1974 it totaled $2.57 billion. This massive shift to support for Israel took place not because U.S. officials were drawn to the just cause of the Israeli state but for cold war political and geostrategic reasons. Israel, a small and fragile state under siege, began to look like an important ally to the American empire because of U.S. dependency on foreign oil and fear of Soviet influence in Arab states.

Today Israel—a country of 6.5 million people—receives 33 percent of the entire foreign-aid budget of the American empire ($3 billion a year). Another 20 percent of the budget goes to Egypt, in part as a payment for not attacking Israel, and Jordan is the third largest recipient (comparable to India!). In short, more than half the budget concerns the security of Israel. The average African receives 10 cents a year from U.S. foreign aid. The average Israeli receives $500 a year. Only 0.2 percent of the U.S. GNP goes to foreign aid—by this measure America ranks last out of the twenty-two wealthiest countries in the world!

A conservative estimate of total U.S. foreign aid to Israel since 1949 is $97.5 billion. Israel has become a military giant (with nuclear weapons) in the Middle East, and yet that military might and the protectorship of the United States that has accompanied all the munitions have not come for free. Israel has paid a price: it has no peace or real security. Historically empires have looked to their allies to assist in their dirty work, and Israel played a key role in some of the most morally indefensible policies of the United States as it waged the cold war: providing arms, training, and intelligence support for the Somoza dictatorship in Nicaragua, the Afrikaner government of apartheid South Africa, UNITA thugs in Angola, and repressive juntas in Guatemala. Like Turkey, Greece, and South Korea, Israel became a frontline U.S. ally, and no other ally in the Middle East yielded such positive results.

As this strategic alliance developed and deepened, American elites and certain powerful factions of American Jewish leadership became so hardened in their partnership that they adopted a "broach no criticisms" position about Israel's actions in the conflict with the Palestinians, a stance that effectively silenced critics, including Jewish critics.

The painful irony is that the most significant and powerful group of Jews outside beleaguered Israel has not been free to engage in a robust debate about the policies of the Israeli government. There are indeed many prophetic Jews out of the 6.1 million Jews in America (1.8 percent of the U.S. population) eager to pursue honest, Socratic questioning of the hard-line position of the U.S.-Israeli alliance, but their voices are marginalized and their motives are often maligned. Mainstream Jewish leadership has suffocated genuine Jewish prophetic views and visions. In this way, the most visible Jewish identity in the Diaspora appears to many, here and abroad, to be an imperial identity whose security resides in military might and the colonial occupation of Palestinians. Yet in regard to domestic policy, American Jews have been the most loyal group—other than black Americans—to support civil rights and civil liberties. Jews have been a pillar for liberal efforts to support social justice for all in America, yet the issue of the Jewish state tends to muzzle their democratic energies.

Through the lens of the Jewish invention of the prophetic, which harkens back to the struggle against Pharaoh's Egypt, this conservative Jewish identity in regard to Israel reeks of imperial idolatry, and it remains in place as long as a grossly simplified Manichaean framework for discussion of the conflict is promulgated. This is a paralyzing framework that posits U.S.-supported, civilized Israelis with their backs against the wall against Arab-supported Palestinian savages who revel in terrorism. This take on the complex situation is so impoverished that it promotes a callousness in denying the extent of Palestinian suffering, in the name of dubious security of Israelis. In short, this myopic viewpoint precludes both justice for Palestinians and security for Israelis.

As Michael C. Staub points out in his recent book, *Torn at the Roots: The Crisis of Jewish Liberalism in Postwar America* (2002), the fierce debates within the Jewish community over Zionism, desegregation, Vietnam, gender relations, and exogamous marriage more and more put prophetic Jews on the defensive. He writes:

Yes, many Jews were, and a considerable number still are, radicals, left-liberals, or more moderate liberals. But without paying attention to intra-Jewish conflict we have no sense of just how embattled these individuals' positions within the community often were, nor of how energetically and creatively anti-left and anti-liberal arguments were put forward by their critics. For example, Jewish activists who invoked the prophetic tradition of Micah, Amos, and Isaiah to cast Judaism as morally bound to antiracist activism and other social justice issues already came under sharp attack in the mid-1950s.

In regard to the Israeli-Palestinian conflict, he notes that, by the 1970s, "it would be hard not to conclude that the hawks had triumphed over the doves. . . . It is crucial to register the on-going vitality of a right-leaning, religiously inflected American Zionism."

The recent history of prophetic American Jews questioning the myopic viewpoint and Manichaean framework of this conflict is appalling. The experience of Breira is revealing. *Breira* is Hebrew for "alternative." In the years 1973 to 1977, this group of prophetic American Jews tried to create a democratic space that allowed serious debate about the fate of Israelis and Palestinians beyond the narrow consensus of mainstream American Jewish leadership—a consensus predicated on *"ein breira"* (there is no alternative to the reigning consensus).

Breira accused the Jewish establishment of a kind of "Israelotry" that blindly worshipped the Israeli state while downplaying Jewish democratic commitments to peace and justice. The group strongly supported the security of Israel and bravely promoted a Palestinian state. Most important, Breira members called for a respectful democratic debate among American Jews regarding the Israeli-Palestinian conflict. And they were viciously attacked and mercilessly crushed—denied membership in local Jewish organizations, forced to quit Breira in order to keep their Hillel rabbi jobs, and cast as self-hating Jews. This antidemocratic response of the mainstream Jewish groups sent chills down the spines of prophetic Jews. For example, the treatment of Rabbi Arthur Waskow was atrocious. His prophetic pro-Israel and pro-Palestine stance was deliberately cast as a terroristic pro-PLO position. He was dubbed a "Jew for Fatah" rather than a concerned rabbi rooted in the rich prophetic tradition of Judaism. Like Rabbi Michael Lerner today, Rabbi Waskow was unfairly labeled a Jewish heretic or traitor. Yet both today persevere against such attacks.

And the present does look more promising. Strong prophetic voices are in fact emerging within the Jewish Diaspora—as well as in Israel—that are putting forward powerful critiques of Israel's handling of the crisis and courageous visions of less violent, more democratic ways forward. New Jewish Agenda, Jewish Peace Lobby, Jewish Peace Network, Americans for Peace Now, *Heeb* magazine, Israel Policy Forum, and especially Rabbi Michael Lerner's *Tikkun* magazine and Tikkun community (headed by Rabbi Lerner, Susannah Heschel, and myself) are slowly beginning to turn the tide against the mainstream Jewish imperial idolatry. These organizations rightly recognize that Israeli colonial occupation of Palestinians and deference to American imperial strategic interests produce neither security for Israel nor justice for Palestinians. Yet these prophetic Jews are up against formidable Jewish establishmentarian forces.

Those forces have sponsored an impressive Jewish civic activism, through a highly successful lobby, to support Israeli government policies and snub prophetic Jewish—and non-Jewish—voices. We democrats must support the right of citizens to organize and influence U.S. foreign or domestic policy. Yet there also must be accountability and responsibility in democratic public life, including vibrant debate and dialogue. Unfortunately, the highly effective Jewish lobby seems to have little interest in such debate and dialogue. Like the attacks against Breira and Rabbi Arthur Waskow, the response to prophetic Jews like Rabbi Michael Lerner and others forecloses meaningful democratic exchange.

The two major groups of the Jewish lobby are the American Israel Public Affairs Committee and the Conference of Presidents of Major American Jewish Organizations. The first group consists of 60,000 members and a staff of 130 and has an annual budget of almost $20 million. Widely known as AIPAC, it focuses on Congress, maintaining an office near Capitol Hill. It mobilizes hard-line Israeli supporters in nearly every congressional district and encourages its members to make significant monetary contributions to candidates of both parties (from conservative Republican Trent Lott to liberal Democrat Hillary Clinton), and it can torpedo candidates who criticize Israeli policies, like Cynthia McKinney in Georgia. The second group is composed of the heads of fifty-one Jewish organizations, including the three largest—the Union of

American Hebrew Congregations (1.5 million Reform Jews and their 900 synagogues), the United Synagogue of Conservative Judaism (1.5 million Conservative Jews and their 760 synagogues), and the Orthodox Union (600,000 Orthodox Jews and their 800 congregations). This group has a staff of six and an annual budget of less than a million dollars. And despite its political and ideological diversity, its leader for the past eighteen years, Malcolm Hoenlein, has been dubbed "the most influential private citizen in American foreign policy" by a former high-ranking U.S. diplomat. His fundamental aim is the security of the Jewish state. But the weight he puts on justice for Palestinians is suspect—even though many prophetic Jews in his organization want both security for Israel and justice for Palestinians. In short, those in the powerful Jewish lobby—though far from monolithic and certainly not an almighty cabal of Zionists who rule the United States or the world (in the vicious language of zealous anti-Semites)—are far to the right of most American Jews and are often contemptuous of prophetic Jewish voices. In fact, their preoccupation with Israel's security at the expense of the Palestinian cry for justice has not only produced little security for Israel but also led many misinformed Jews down an imperial path that suffocates their own prophetic heritage.

This suffocation is seen most clearly in the major sectors of the mass media. Mortimer Zuckerman, the new head of the Conference of Presidents of Major American Jewish Organizations, owns *U.S. News & World Report* and the *New York Daily News*. Martin Peretz, editor in chief and co-owner of the *New Republic*, is a defender of hard-line Israeli policies toward the Palestinians. The Sulzbergers, the more sophisticated and open-minded Jewish family who publish the *New York Times*, house the unofficial dean of American foreign-affairs journalism, the bestselling author Thomas Friedman, whose misrepresentations of the Middle East are legion (yet whose call to pull back on Israeli settlements is courageous). Needless to add, the far-reaching influence of the non-Jewish Rupert Murdoch (*New York Post, Weekly Standard,* Fox News Channel) is enormous. He is a stalwart of the imperial U.S.-Israeli lobby.

The dominant voices of the American Jewish lobby have, in fact, so eviscerated their own prophetic Jewish tradition that they have even embraced the support of conservative evangelical Christians. How ironic it is to see this Jewish lobby fuse with right-wing evangelical Christians whose anti-Semitism, past and present, is notorious, and whose support for Israel is based on the idea that the Jewish state paves the way for the Second Coming of Christ. The recent controversy over Mel Gibson's film *The Passion of the Christ* reveals the absurdity of this unholy alliance. To worship the golden calf of power and might is one thing. To unite with the heirs of the fundamental source of anti-Judaism in last two thousand years of Jewish history—whose literal readings of the New Testament reek of anti-Semitic views—is to reveal the depths of establishmentarian Jewish capitulation to the worst of the American empire.

The greatest Jewish philosopher of the twentieth century—Franz Rosenzweig—put the critique of idolatry at the center of his thought, as shown in Leora Batnitzky's brilliant *Idolatry and Representation: The Philosophy of Rosenzweig Reconsidered* (2000):

The Jewishness of a Jew is done an injustice if it is put on the same level as his nationality. . . . There is no "relationship" between one's Jewishness and one's humanity that needs to be discovered, puzzled out, experienced, or created. . . . As a Jew one is a human being, as a human being a Jew. . . . Strange as it may sound to the obtuse ears of a nationalist, being a Jew is no limiting barrier that cuts Jews off from someone who is limited by being something else.

Rosenzweig's powerful critique of Zionism—alongside his un-equivocal support for Jewish security—is relevant for our time. He knew that the all-too-human idolizing of land and power trumps prophetic commitments to justice and yields little genuine security. This kind of idolatry tends to encourage imperial ambitions and colonial aims, as noted by Ahad Ha'am, the towering Jewish critic, more than one hundred years ago after his visit to Palestine. He wrote:

Some of the newcomers, to our shame, describe themselves as "future colonialists." . . . They were slaves in their diasporas, and suddenly they find themselves with unlimited freedom. . . . This sudden change has planted despotic tendencies in their hearts, as always happens to former slaves. They deal with the Arabs with hostility and cruelty, trespass un-justly, beat them shamefully for no sufficient reason, and even boast about their actions. There is no one to stop the flood and put an end to this despicable and dangerous tendency.

Similarly, prophetic Jewish giants like Albert Einstein and Leo Baeck, who in 1948 spoke "in the name of principles which have been the most significant contributions of the Jewish people to humanity," have chastised the myopic approach to the conflict. As they wrote in a letter to the *New York Times* in 1948:

> Both Arab and Jewish extremists are today recklessly pushing Palestine into a futile war. While believing in the defense of legitimate claims, these extremists on each side play into each other's hands. In this reign of terror, the needs and desires of the common man in Palestine are ignored. . . . We believe that any constructive solution is possible only if it is based on the concern for the welfare and cooperation of both Jews and Arabs in Palestine.

They knew that a new democratic Jewish identity must be forged in the Diaspora that shatters all imperial mentalities and unleashes the prophetic energies of decent, justice-loving Jews and non-Jews. This democratic identity must mirror the very realities that have allowed Jewish success and upward mobility in America— rights and liberties, merit and respect for all in a democratic experiment. Would American Jews elect to live in an America that bans interfaith marriage, guarantees a Christian majority to keep minorities as second-class citizens, and rules brutally over its adjacent neighbors whose property they daily annex? Does not the Jewish state ban marriage between Jews and non-Jews, discriminate against its Arab citizens, and subjugate Palestinians under occupation?

American Jews have been in the forefront of the fight for the rights and liberties of oppressed peoples, especially blacks. Where are those same prophetic voices when it comes to the rights of Palestinians within Israel and under Israeli occupation? This is a moment when progressive Jews are under severe attack and severe test. If ever there was a time in which the best voices of the Jewish world should be heard, it is now. The connection of much of American Jewish power to the most conservative elements in the American elite has allowed a downplaying of the suffering of the Palestinian people and a willingness to view the lives of the Palestinians as of less value than those of Jews or Americans. Thus we have the need to be at the same time unequivocal in our support for the security of Israel and fully committed to ending the subjugation of the Palestinians. Prophetic Jews can maintain both the demand for Israeli security and the call for an end to occupation, while also joining with non-Jews who are ready to support them. They can open up possibilities for a very important kind of progressive movement.

The tragic irony is that the deep faith of American and Israeli Jews in the American empire is itself idolatrous and dangerous. It is idolatrous because it makes the U.S. helicopter gunships that patrol the Palestinian West Bank and the U.S.-supported wall that separates Palestinians from Israel the dominant imperial symbols of an Israel founded in the name of the Israelite prophets. It is dangerous because it views America as the Jewish promised land, bereft of its own deep anti-Semitic impulses. Yet the truth is that just as the American empire chose to favor Israel for political and geostrategic reasons, it can abandon Israel for the same reasons. And if an oil-rich Arab country could do imperial America's dirty work better than Israel at a lower cost and with less controversy, Israel might well be sold down the river.

Is there not a long and ugly history of Jews in the Diaspora—Spain, Egypt, Germany—succumbing to false security and assimilationist illusions as they deferred to respective imperial authorities? Is America so different? Do the depths of anti-Semitism in Western civilization and Christian-dominated societies not reach to the heart of America? What will happen when American imperial elites must choose between oil and Israel? Cannot these elites manipulate anti-Semitic sentiments among the American citizenry the same way they fan and fuel other xenophobic fears for purposes of expediency? The challenge of democrats is to keep track of *all* forms of bigotry—including anti-Semitism—and to unsettle the sleepwalking among the comfortable. This means working with and alongside our Jewish fellow citizens in forging a new Jewish democratic identity here and abroad.

Just as a new Jewish democratic identity can draw from the rich prophetic tradition of Judaism, so a new Islamic democratic identity can, and must, emerge from the rich prophetic tradition of Islam. Recent efforts to embark on democratic projects in Afghanistan and Iraq are salutary, but they must not be guided by imperial aims or informed by simplistic understandings of the

Islamic tradition. Furthermore, any attempt to democratize Islamic states or to Socratize Islam must be conversant with their recent imperial past.

The recent waves of Islamic revitalization movements—be they fundamentalist or not—are a quest for a new identity of subjugated Muslims in response to failed secular nationalist experiments. These nationalist experiments—Nasser in Egypt, the shah in Iran, Saddam in Iraq—were unable to create and sustain a workable identity for Islamic subjects in the aftermath of imperial subjugation. And their respective links with the Soviet and American empires during the cold war widened the gap between the thuggish rulers and their Muslim subjects. With the collapse of repressive secular nationalism at the top, the Islamic revival mobilized the masses and gained state power. This revival was guided by a particular kind of Islam—a clerical Islam rooted in the religious identity of people and responsive to the pervasive anxieties unleashed by the failure of secular nationalist ideology in the wake of a colonial past.

In this sense, recent Islamic revitalization movements are not mindless revolts against modernity or blind expressions of hatred toward America. Their eager appropriations of modern technology (possibly including nuclear weapons) or selective infatuations with American culture (especially music) undercut such fashionable clichés. Rather, turbulent rumblings in the contemporary Islamic world—with a population of one billion people—are fueled by fears of cultural deracination and fanned by hopes for material security. The quest for an Islamic identity shuns the uprootedness and restlessness of the modern West and the licentiousness and avariciousness of the American empire. It is similar to any other modern fundamentalist response to certain aspects of modernity, be it Christian, Judaic, or tribalistic. Yet religious traditions are here to stay, and the question is how to support prophetic voices and forge democratic identities within them in our day.

Identity in the highly developed world is often a subject of leisurely conversation and academic banter. In the poor developing world, identity is a matter of life and death. Identity has to do with who one is and how one moves from womb to tomb—the elemental desires for protection, recognition, and association in a cold and cruel world. Like the traditions of belief of most peoples of color in the Americas, religious traditions of oppressed peoples in the Middle East, Africa, and Asia posit the modern West itself as an idol to be suspicious of and distant from. Their major exposure to and encounter with the modern West was its imperial face—a boot on one's neck. And although they might long for the conveniences and comforts of modern capitalist technologies, they are mindful of Western capitalism's sterling rhetoric and oppressive practices and they abhor the pervasive materialistic individualism and destructive hedonism. This is not a childish rejection of modernity but rather a wise attempt to enter the modern world on one's own terms.

When modern imperial ideologies have dehumanized you and modern enterprises have exploited your labor, postcolonial situations become occasions to assert your sense of self and culture even when doing so appears backward to those who have been riding your back. Glib imitation of the West is suicide—even if recasting Islamic identity is painful, as profoundly and poignantly revealed in the great modern Islamic literature. The paradigmatic literary figures of Samba Diallo in Cheikh Hamidou Kane's inimitable *Ambiguous Adventure* (1983), Mustafa Sa'eed in Tayeb Salih's powerful *Season of Migration to the North* (1969), Ken Bugul in Mariétou M'Baye's classic *The Abandoned Baobab* (1991), and Driss Ferdi in Driss Chraibi's canonical *The Simple Past* (1983) all lay bare the inescapable need to confront their Islamic tradition.

This noteworthy body of literature—much of it centered in the African Islamic world—deserves much more attention for those concerned about Islam, modernity, and democracy. In stark contrast to renowned literary figures like Salman Rushdie and V. S. Naipaul, these writers are sympathetic to the Islamic sources of their modern identity and to the modern sources of their Islamic identity. These works explore the profound alienation from both sources, and the necessity of building on both sources—all against the background of the West as imperial agent. As Kane writes in *Ambiguous Adventure:*

> The new school shares at the same time the characteristics of cannon and of magnet. From the cannon it draws its efficacy as an arm of combat. Better than the cannon, it makes the conquest permanent. The cannon compels the body, the school bewitches the soul. Where the cannon has made a pit of ashes and of death, in the sticky mold of which men would not have rebounded from the ruins, the new school establishes peace. The morning of rebirth will be a morning of benediction through the appeasing virtue of the new school.

From the magnet, the school takes its radiating force. It is bound up with a new order, as a magnetic stone is bound up with a field. The upheaval of the life of man within this new order is similar to the overturn of certain physical laws in a magnetic field. Men are seen to be composing themselves, conquered, along the lines of invisible forces. Disorder is organized, rebellion is appeased, the mornings of resentment resound with songs of universal thanksgiving.

This Islamic quest for a modern identity is situated between Good Friday and Easter, between a past of deep imperial wounds and a forward-looking resurrection. To erase the modern West is to ignore the dark predicament of the Islamic present. To wipe the traditions of Islam away would be to render themselves a blank carbon copy of a modern West that has no room or place for their complexity and humanity. Democracy matters must confront this Islamic identity crisis critically and sympathetically. In other words, there can be no democracy in the Islamic world without a recasting of Islamic identity. This new modern identity that fuses Islam and democracy has not even been glimpsed by most westerners. So it behooves us to proceed in a self-critical and open manner.

The delicate dialogue between the modern West and the Islamic world should be neither a crude clash of civilizations nor an imposition of one upon the other. Rather it should be a Socratic process of examining a rich past of cultural cross-fertilization. Just as there is a long Judeo-Christian tradition, there is a long Judeo-Islamic tradition. The role of Islamic figures in the history of Judaic and Christian thought is immense. And the prophetic energies in Judaism and Christianity have been appropriated by many prophetic Islamic thinkers. These energies provide a hope for new democratic possibilities. This treacherous road has already been trod by towering Islamic intellectuals—like Fatima Mernissi, Mohamed Abid al-Jabri, Abdokarim Soroush, Mohamed Arkoun, Nawal El Saadawi, Anouar Majid, Tariq Ramadan, Khaled Abou El-Fadl, and, above all, Mahmoud Mohamed Taha—who all question, and examine, the modern West and Islamic traditions in order to forge a new democratic vision in the Muslim world. As Khaled Abou El-Fadl boldly proclaims in his article "Islam and the Challenge of Democracy" in the *Boston Review* (April–May 2003):

A central conceptual problem is that modern democracy evolved over centuries within the distinctive context of post-Reformation, market-oriented Christian Europe. Does it make sense to look for points of contact in a remarkably different context? My answer begins from the premise that democracy and Islam are defined in the first instance by their underlying moral values and the attitudinal commitments of their adherents—not by the ways that those values and commitments have been applied. If we focus on those fundamental moral values, I believe, we will see that the tradition of Islamic political thought contains both interpretive and practical possibilities that can be developed into a democratic sys-

tem. To be sure, these doctrinal potentialities may remain unrealized: without will power, inspired vision,
and moral commitment there can be no democracy
in Islam. But Muslims, for whom Islam is the author-
itative frame of reference, can come to the conviction
that democracy is an ethical good, and that the pursuit
of this good does not require abandoning Islam.

The first step in discerning prophetic energies in Islam and
forging an Islamic democratic identity is to put forward a persuasive genealogy of the subtle developments of Islamic legal thought
(Usul al-fiqh and fiqh), theology (Kalam), mysticism (Tasawwuf),
and philosophy (falsafa). This is an enormous task. This genealogy
would lay bare the variety of interpretations and possibilities of
thinking about Islam in relation to democratic practices. For example, those who stress Islamic law often espouse very different
views than those who highlight Islamic mysticism. The dominant
tendency in the Islamic revitalization movements today is to put a
wholesale premium on Islamic law—Islam as Shari'a. This emphasis already reduces the complexities and possibilities of Islam.
This is especially so in regard to the crucial question of contemporary Islamic women, since patriarchy is an integral part of
Islamic law.

Yet there are both prelegalistic and postlegalistic forms of Islam
that sidestep this patriarchal limit in Islam. It is the legalistic conception of Islam that often authorizes an antidemocratic rule of
Muslim jurists. This version of Islam is dominant in the world
today, but it does not exhaust the forms of Islam in the past, pres-

ent, or future. Clerical Islam and legalistic Islam have a history, and their history resurfaces with power at specific moments. The present form of clerical Islam is an authoritarian effort to secure an Islamic identity and to run modern nation-states given the collapse of secular nationalism and the defeat of earlier European imperialisms in the Islamic world. Like rabbinical Judaism or Catholic Christianity, clerical Islam is in no way the essence of Islam—or its only form. Similarly, Islam, like all religions, has always incorporated non-Islamic and nonreligious sources that often appear to the believer to be purely Islamic. No modern religion can survive without learning from modern science, modern politics, and modern culture. Every modern religion accepts Newton's law of gravity, Weber's role of bureaucracies, and contemporary musical instruments in its rituals. All religions are polyvalent— subject to multiple interpretations under changing circumstances. Islam must be understood, by both non-Muslims and Muslims, as a fluid repertoire of ways of being a Muslim, not a dogmatic stipulation of rules that govern one's life. Or, to put it another way, every dogmatic set of rules now espoused by the dominant clerics was once a challenge to an older dogmatic set of rules.

The new dogma has simply become so routinized and ossified that it conceals its former contingency and insurgency. In this way, even to be a dogmatic traditionalist is to be part of a dynamic history and ever-changing tradition. This understanding of the fluidity of Islam is required in order for a democratic Islam to challenge the authority of Muslim clerics and Islamic jurists who attempt to naturalize and fossilize their prevailing edicts and decrees. The clerics and jurists themselves constitute forms of authority that result from earlier struggles over the role of clerics and who can be a jurist. The fundamental aim of authoritarian clerical Islam today is to procure an identity and secure a stable society over against the bombardments of the modern West, and the internal failures of past nationalist and imperial regimes.

The key to Socratizing Islam is to understand precisely what kinds of authority present-day clerical Islam was a response to and to show that the new democratic Islamic responses to clerical Islam can promote Islamic aims in a more spiritually and politically effective manner. In short, modern clerical Islam was a response to the imperial European authorities that degraded Islamic religion, plundered Islamic resources, and cast the Islamic way of being and living as inferior to that of the modern West. The dominant secular response to imperial Europe was nationalism (be it Arab, Asian, or African nationalism)—itself an imitation of European nationalisms that revolted against empires inside Europe (like that in nineteenth-century Germany and the Italian nationalist revolt against Napoleon). This secular nationalism has failed in the Islamic world. And the grand example of Turkey—where secular nationalism, the religion of the elites, is imposed by an autonomous and repressive military on an Islamic populace—is what the Islamic world wants to avoid. (Ayatollah Khomeini's clerical Islam overthrew the shah's U.S.-backed nationalism in 1979 for the same reason.) Why? Because, like Israel, Turkey is a satellite country of the American empire generally willing to do imperial America's dirty work in the Middle East, even as America looks the other way regarding Turkey's vicious treatment of Islamic Kurds.

Many Muslims see Turkey's model as a form of U.S.-supported, anti-Islamic nationalism to be shunned and rejected. Turkey's militaristic nationalism supported by the American empire represses Kurdish nationalism with a vengeance. This replay of European nationalist ideologies does not bode well for the Islamic world. The same dynamic holds in Pakistan, Indonesia, Morocco, and Egypt— all allies of imperial America. It is no accident that when these countries, like Israel, violate international law, imperial America looks the other way. The examples of Turkey's seizure of two-fifths of Cyprus, Indonesia's of East Timor, Morocco's of Western Sahara, and Israel's of Palestinian lands make the point. Such colonial conquests do not generate a mumbling word from imperial America in the United Nations or anywhere else. Only when the interests of the American empire are at stake—as in Saddam Hussein's barbaric actions in Kuwait or Kim Jong Il's vicious threats in Korea—does U.S. moral rhetoric about freedom surface. The repressive clerics in the autocratic Islamic states know this—and they are right. Yet even as this clerical Islam is attractive to many Islamic peoples in comparison to failed secular nationalism, this same clerical Islam is ruthlessly and horribly autocratic and is suffocating the democratic energies in the region.

Therefore, the present task is to undermine the authority of the Muslim clerics on Islamic and democratic grounds. Western-style democracy has no future in the Islamic world. The damage has been done, the wounds are deep, and the die has been cast by the hypocritical European and nihilistic American imperial elites. There is simply no way to turn back the hands of time. The West had its chance and blew it. Yet the future of democracy in the Islamic world may be bright if democratic notions of voice and rights, community and liberties, rotation of elites and autonomous civic spaces are couched in Islamic terms and traditions. Western-style democracies—themselves in need of repair—are but one member of the family of democracy. Yet all democracies share certain common features, such as the voices of the demos; rotating elites; free expression of religion, culture, and politics; and uncoerced spaces for civic life. But we can encourage the Socratizing of Islam and the prophetizing of the Muslim populace even as we dismantle empire at home.

There are three basic efforts to democratize the Islamic world by Muslims themselves. The first endeavor is to show that Islamic legalistic conceptions of justice (*'adl,* or procedural justice, and *ma'ruf,* or substantive justice) are compatible with democratic conceptions of justice. This is a fascinating and pioneering attempt to show that the Qur'an can be interpreted to support democracy. The complex relation of justice to revelation looms large. Does justice flow from divine revelation, or does justice exist apart from divine revelation? Furthermore, is justice an abstract ideal that puts forth rules that regulate a society (as the great political philosopher John Rawls would argue), or is justice one virtue among others to be balanced with them in the lived experience of Islamic peoples? What if these other virtues—like piety and temperance—downplay, contradict, or curtail democratic conceptions of justice? The pioneering work of Khaled Abou El-Fadl here in America best exemplifies this important tendency in contemporary Islam, in works such as *The Place of Tolerance in Islam.* His article in the *Boston Review* is a good place to begin:

A case for democracy presented from within Islam must accept the idea of God's sovereignty: it cannot substitute popular sovereignty for divine sovereignty, but must instead show how popular sovereignty—with its idea that citizens have rights and a correlative responsibility to pursue justice with mercy—expresses God's authority, properly understood. Similarly, it cannot reject the idea that God's law is given prior to human action, but must show how democratic lawmaking respects that priority.

The second effort does away with all appeals to Islamic law—it is an Islam without Shari'a. As noted earlier, Islamic women often promote this endeavor in order to undercut the deeply patriarchal character and content of Islamic law. On this view, Islam is more an open-ended way of life and less a set of rules to obey. It harkens back to the early days before the rise of clerical Islam. It also allows a more free-flowing connection with democratic sensibilities, much like the practice of tolerance in the first Islamic state in 622, established by the Prophet Muhammad himself in his compact of Medina, which insisted on mutual respect and civility between Jews and Muslims. He enacted a constitutional rule that was based on a principled agreement between the Muhajirun (Muslim immigrants from Mecca), the Ansar (indigenous Muslims of Medina), and the Yahud (Jews). This federation authorized that the different communities were equal in rights and duties. In this way, the first Islamic state stands in stark contrast to the anti-Semitic practices of most of the autocratic Islamic states of our day.

The last major effort is found in the rich and revolutionary writings of Mahmoud Mohamed Taha (himself murdered by the Nimeiri regime in Sudan for his visionary and courageous works). For example, in his manifesto, *The Second Message of Islam,* Taha conceives of Islam as a holistic way of life that promotes freedom—the overcoming of fear—in order to pursue a loving and wise life. As in the second effort, he and his disciple Abdullahi Ahmed An-Na'im discard the Shari'a and replace it with the Meccan revelation. Taha's conception of the good society rests upon economic equality (egalitarian sharing of wealth), political equality (political sharing in decisions), and social equality (no discrimination based on color, faith, race, or sex in order to provide equal opportunity for cultural refinement). Similar to the Prophet Muhammad, Taha revels in difference—or promotes diversity—in order to constitute a more fair and equal society. Anouar Majid's superb text *Unveiling Traditions: Postcolonial Islam in a Polycentric World* is a must-read. In that book he writes:

> My examination of postcolonial theory and the Arab identity deployed by nationalists to counter imperialism might . . . help explain why a progressively defined Islam—one that is democratically available to all—may be a desirable option for Muslim peoples. . . . Islamic cultures—like many of the world's cultural traditions—could help "provincialize" the West and offer other ways to be in the world. . . .
>
> More broadly, this book tries to challenge secular academics to include the world's nonsecular expres-

sions as equally worthy of consideration and valid al-
ternatives, and Muslim scholars to rethink their at-
tachments to texts and canons that have obscured the
egalitarian and viable legacies of Islam.

At the moment, those views are but voices in the wilderness.
Yet they are also a delicious foretaste of the new wave of Socratic
questioning, prophetic witness, and tragicomic hope ascending
within the Islamic world. These prophetic voices constitute a leaven
in the Islamic loaf—and much hangs on whether social forces in
the Islamic world can enact their democratic visions. And there is
more to come—calls to reconfigure institutional structures that jet-
tison the colonial nation-states and establish more cosmopolitan
educational systems that highlight the rich links between the
Judeo-Christian, Judeo-Islamic, Christian-Islamic, and secular
traditions. The future of democracy matters in the world depends
in part on these heroic and imaginative efforts—and not only in
Islamic regions. Dismantling empire is a multifaceted affair, and
our gallant attempts to do so require all the vision and courage we
can muster here and abroad.

Yet the colossal presence of the American empire in the Jewish
and Islamic world—especially its dependence on oil—muddies the
water. It silently condones autocratic Islamic states and openly
green-lights Israeli hard-line colonial policies. And even as it em-
barks on an imperial-monitored democratization in Iraq, its heavy
hand is felt among those who are glad that the dictatorial Hussein
is gone, but suspicious of U.S. strategies and goals. The ugly effects
of this heavy-handedness were expressed eloquently by the mod-

erate Iraqi cleric Ghazi Ajil al-Yawar, who is quoted in an article in the *New York Times Magazine:* "The U.S. is using excessive power. They round up people in a very humiliating way, by putting bags over their faces in front of their families. In our society, this is like rape. The Americans are using collective punishment by jailing relatives. What is the difference from Saddam?" The recent revelations of U.S. atrocities in Iraqi prisons (especially Abu Ghraib) confirm this heavy-handedness.

Needless to say, the fall of any nihilistic gangster who rules with an iron hand is salutary. New democratic possibilities arise. But a subtle understanding of the imperial past of the region, a complex grasp of the Islamic and Jewish quests for identity, and a genuine commitment to deep democracy are required for substantive justice and peace for Muslims and Jews.

The ultimate irony may be that the most fertile seeds for democracy matters in the Islamic world can be found in the civic life of the Palestinians and Kurds—the most subjugated peoples in the region, forced to survive and thrive without a nation-state. Beneath the autocratic rule of Arafat looms a vital network of norms and trust that could give birth to democratic practices in the aftermath of Israeli occupation. Ordinary Palestinians could well be the most democratically inclined Muslims in the world. They have been used by Arab elites to trash Israel and compete for imperial American aid and attention. These same Palestinians may be democratic pioneers who inspire the democratization of the Islamic peoples in the region.

Similarly, Kurds in northern Iraq and Turkey have sustained democratic practices in the face of atrocious repression and vicious attacks. At the moment, they have proven to be the most democratic Muslims in the world. The American empire has closed its eyes to Kurdish oppression by its ally Turkey and only recently opened its eyes to the long-standing Kurdish democratic practices in northern Iraq. Are there lessons to be learned here? Can the anti-imperial aspirations of Palestinians and Kurds sidestep autocratic forms of secular nationalism and Islamic revitalization? Can they thereby unleash democratic energies if the U.S. imperial presence is lifted, the Israeli occupation ended, and Kurdish self-determination allowed to flourish? And would not pioneering Palestinians and Kurds be inspired by the magnificent democratic achievements of Israel itself if the Jewish state emerged out of the shadow of U.S. imperialism and took its rightful vanguard place among democratic national experiments in the region?

5

THE CRISIS OF CHRISTIAN IDENTITY IN AMERICA

Our solutions and decisions are relative, because they are related to the fragmentary and frail measure of our faith. We have not found and shall not find—until Christ comes again—a Christian in history whose faith so ruled his life that every thought was brought into subjection to it and every moment and place was for him in the kingdom of God. Each one has encountered the mountain he could not move, the demon he could not exorcise. . . . All our faith is fragmentary, though we do not all have the same fragments of faith.

—H. RICHARD NIEBUHR, *Christ and Culture* (1951)

I must take the responsibility for how, mark my word, *how* I react to the forces that impinge upon my life, forces that are not responsive to my will, my desire, my ambition, my dream, my hope—forces that don't know that I'm here. But I know I'm here. And I decide whether I will say yes, or no, and make it hold. This indeed is the free man, and this is anticipated in the genius of the dogma of freedom as a manifestation of the soul of America, born in what to me is one of the greatest of the great experiments in human relations.

—HOWARD THURMAN, *America in Search of a Soul* (1976)

The religious threats to democratic practices abroad are much easier to talk about than those at home. Just as demagogic and antidemocratic fundamentalisms have gained too much prominence in both Israel and the Islamic world, so too has a fundamentalist strain of Christianity gained far too much power in our political system, and in the hearts and minds of citizens. This Christian fundamentalism is exercising an undue influence over our government policies, both in the Middle East crisis and in the domestic sphere, and is violating fundamental principles enshrined in the Constitution; it is also providing support and "cover" for the imperialist aims of empire. The three dogmas that are leading to the imperial devouring of democracy in America—free-market fundamentalism, aggressive militarism, and escalating authoritarianism—are often justified by the religious rhetoric of this Christian fundamentalism. And perhaps most ironically—and sadly—this fundamentalism is subverting the most profound, seminal teachings of Christianity, those being that we should live with humility, love our neighbors, and do unto others as we would have them do unto us. Therefore, even as we turn a critical eye on the fundamentalisms at play in the Middle East, the genuine democrats and democratic Christians among us must unite in opposition to this hypocritical, antidemocratic fundamentalism at home. The battle for the soul of American democracy is, in large part, a battle for the soul of American Christianity, because the dominant forms of Christian fundamentalism are a threat to the tolerance and openness necessary for sustaining any democracy. Yet the best of

American Christianity has contributed greatly to preserving and expanding American democracy. The basic distinction between Constantinian Christianity and prophetic Christianity is crucial for the future of American democracy.

Surveys have shown that 80 percent of Americans call themselves Christians, 72 percent expect the Second Coming of Christ, and 40 percent say they speak to the Christian God on intimate terms at least twice a week. America is undeniably a highly religious country, and the dominant religion by far is Christianity, and much of American Christianity is a form of Constantinian Christianity. In American Christendom, the fundamental battle between democracy and empire is echoed in the struggle between this Constantinian Christianity and prophetic Christianity.

This battle between prophetic Christians and Constantinian Christians goes back to the first centuries of the Christian movement that emerged out of Judaism. The Roman emperor Constantine's incorporation of Christianity within the empire gave Christianity legitimacy and respectability but robbed it of the prophetic fervor of Jesus and the apocalyptic fire of that other Jew-turned-Christian named Paul. Until Constantine converted to Christianity in AD 312 and decriminalized it with the Edict of Milan in 313, and his successor Theodosius I made Christianity the official religion of the empire, the Christian movement had been viciously persecuted by the imperial Romans, primarily because the growing popularity of the Christian message of humility, and of equality among men, was understood as a threat to Roman imperial rule.

Jesus was so brutally executed by the Roman empire—crucifixion being the empire's most horrific and terrifying tactic of punishing offenders to its rule—precisely because his preaching of the coming of the kingdom of God was seen by the Romans as danger-ously subversive of the authoritarianism and militarism of the Roman state. Ironically, Jesus's message of love and justice pro-moted a separation of his prophetic witness from Caesar's author-ity—"render unto Caesar what is Caesar's," Christ said. Yet the nihilistic imperialism of the Romans was so power-hungry that it couldn't tolerate the growing popularity of the Christian sects. When the growth of the religion couldn't be stopped, the Roman empire co-opted it. With Constantine's conversion, a terrible co-joining of church and state was institutionalized from which the religion and many of its victims, especially Jews, have suffered ever since. Constantinian Christianity has always been at odds with the prophetic legacy of Jesus Christ. Constantine himself seems to have converted to Christianity partly out of political strategy and impe-rial exigency, and then proceeded to use the cloak of Christianity for his own purposes of maintaining power.

As the Christian church became increasingly corrupted by state power, religious rhetoric was often used to justify imperial aims and conceal the prophetic heritage of Christianity. Immediately after his conversion, Constantine targeted numerous Christian sects for annihilation—such as the Gnostics and other groups that questioned the books of the Old Testament—as he consolidated power by creating one imperial version of Christianity. The cor-ruption of a faith fundamentally based on tolerance and compas-sion by the strong arm of imperial authoritarianism invested Christianity with an insidious schizophrenia with which it has been battling ever since. This terrible merger of church and state has been behind so many of the church's worst violations of Christian love and justice—from the barbaric crusades against Jews and Muslims, to the horrors of the Inquisition and the ugly bigotry against women, people of color, and gays and lesbians.

This same religious schizophrenia has been a constant feature of American Christianity. The early American branch of the Christian movement—the Puritans—consisted of persecuted victims of the British empire in search of liberty and security. On the one hand, they laid the foundations for America's noble anti-imperialist struggle against the British empire. On the other hand, they enacted the imperialist subordination of Amerindians. Their democratic sensibilities were intertwined with their authoritarian sentiments. The American democratic experiment would have been inconceivable without the fervor of Christians, yet strains of Constantinianism were woven into the fabric of America's Christian identity from the start. Constantinian strains of American Christianity have been on the wrong side of so many of our social troubles, such as the dogmatic justification of slavery and the parochial defense of women's inequality. It has been the prophetic Christian tradition, by contrast, that has so often pushed for social justice.

When conservative Christians argue today for state-sponsored religious schools, when they throw their tacit or more overt support behind antiabortion zealots or homophobic crusaders who preach hatred (a few have even killed in the name of their belief), they are being Constantinian Christians. These Constantinian Christians fail to appreciate their violation of Christian love and justice because Constantinian Christianity in America places such a strong emphasis on personal conversion, individual piety, and philanthropic service and has lost its fervor for the suspicion of worldly authorities and for doing justice in the service of the most vulnerable among us, which are central to the faith. These energies are rendered marginal to their Christian identity.

Most American Constantinian Christians are unaware of their imperialistic identity because they do not see the parallel between the Roman empire that put Jesus to death and the American empire that they celebrate. As long as they can worship freely and pursue the American dream, they see the American government as a force for good and American imperialism as a desirable force for spreading that good. They proudly profess their allegiance to the flag and the cross not realizing that just as the cross was a bloody indictment of the Roman empire, it is a powerful critique of the American empire, and they fail to acknowledge that the cozy relation between their Christian leaders and imperial American rulers may mirror the intimate ties between the religious leaders and imperial Roman rulers who crucified their Savior.

I have no doubt that most of these American Constantinian Christians are sincere in their faith and pious in their actions. But they are relatively ignorant of the crucial role they play in sponsoring American imperial ends. Their understanding of American history is thin and their grasp of Christian history is spotty, which leaves them vulnerable to manipulation by Christian leaders and misinformation by imperial rulers. The Constantinian Christian support of the pervasive disinvestment in urban centers and cutbacks in public education and health care, as well as their emphatic defense of the hard-line policies of the Israeli government, has much to do with the cozy alliance of Constantinian Christian leaders with the political elites beholden to corporate interests who provide shelter for cronyism. In short, they sell their precious souls for a mess of imperial pottage based on the false belief that they are simply being true to the flag and the cross. The very notion that the prophetic legacy of the grand victim of the Roman empire—Jesus Christ—requires critique of and resistance to American imperial power hardly occurs to them.

These American Constantinian Christians must ask themselves, Does not the vast concentration of so much power and might breed arrogance and hubris? Do not the Old Testament prophets and teachings of Jesus suggest, at the least, a suspicion of such unrivaled and unaccountable wealth and status? Are not empires the occasion of idolatry run amok? Most Christians, including Constantinian ones, are appalled by the ugly AIDS epidemic in Africa—thirty million now—and around the world (forty million). Why has the response of the American empire to this crisis been abysmal? Doesn't the interest of drug companies and their influence on the U.S. government hamper our ability to discover or make available cheap drugs for our ailing fellow human beings? Is it not obvious that the U.S. response would be much different if AIDS victims were white heterosexual upper-middle-class men in Europe or America? Must Christians respond solely through private charities in this disastrous emergency? The response to the AIDS crisis is but one example of the moral callousness of imperial rulers that should upset any Christian. Were not subjugated Jews and later persecuted Christians in the early Roman empire treated in such inhumane and unacceptable ways?

In criticizing the Constantinianism in American Christianity, however, we must not lose sight of the crucial role of prophetic Christianity as a force for democratic good in our history. The values engendered by Christian belief were crucial in fueling first the democratic energy out of which the early religious settlers founded nascent democratic projects and then the indignation with the abuses of the British empire that drove the American Revolution. And the Founders took great pains to establish guarantees of religious freedom in the Constitution out of a deep conviction about the indispensable role of religion in civic life. The most influential social movements for justice in America have been led by prophetic Christians: the abolitionist, women's suffrage, and trade-union movements in the nineteenth century and the civil rights movement in the twentieth century. Though the Constantinian Christianity that has gained so much influence today is undermining the fundamental principles of our democracy regarding the proper role of religion in the public life of a democracy, the prophetic strains in American Christianity have done battle with imperialism and social injustice all along and represent the democratic ideal of religion in public life. This prophetic Christianity adds a moral fervor to our democracy that is a very good thing. It also holds that we must embrace those outside of the Christian faith and act with empathy toward them. This prophetic Christianity is an ecumenical force for good, and if we are to revitalize the democratic energies of the country, we must reassert the vital legitimacy of this prophetic Christianity in our public life, such as the principles of public service, care for the poor, and separation of church and state that this Christianity demands. And we must oppose the intrusions of the fundamentalist Christianity that has so flagrantly violated those same democratic principles.

Most American Christians have little knowledge of many of the most powerful voices in the rich prophetic tradition in American Christianity. They are unfamiliar with the theologian Walter Rauschenbusch, who in his *Christianity and the Social Crisis* (1907) and numerous other influential books was the primary voice of the Social Gospel movement at the turn of the last century. As the industrial engines of the American empire ramped up, leading to the excesses of the Gilded Age, this theological movement perceived that industrial capitalism and its attendant urbanization brought with them inherent social injustices. Its adherents spoke out against the abuse of workers by managements that were not sufficiently constrained by either morality or government regulation. As Rauschenbusch eloquently wrote:

> Individual sympathy and understanding has been our chief reliance in the past for overcoming the differences between the social classes. The feelings and principles implanted by Christianity have been a powerful aid in that direction. But if this sympathy diminishes by the widening of the social chasm, what hope have we?

With the flourishing of American industrialism, our society was becoming corrupted by capitalist greed, Rauschenbusch warned, and Christians had a duty to combat the consequent injustices.

Most American Christians have forgotten or have never learned about the pioneering work of Dorothy Day and the Catholic Worker Movement, which she founded in 1933 during the Great Depression to bring relief to the homeless and the poor. Day set up a House of Hospitality in the slums of New York City and founded the newspaper *Catholic Worker* because she believed that

> by fighting for better conditions, by crying out un-
> ceasingly for the rights of the workers, of the poor, of
> the destitute—the rights of the worthy and the un-
> worthy poor . . . we can to a certain extent change the
> world; we can work for the oasis, the little cell of joy
> and peace in a harried world.

Some of these prophetic Christians have been branded radicals and faced criminal prosecution. During the national trauma of the Vietnam War, the Jesuit priests and brothers Philip and Daniel Berrigan led antiwar activities, with Daniel founding the group Clergy and Laity Concerned about Vietnam. The brothers organized sit-ins and teach-ins against the war and led many protests, notoriously breaking into Selective Service offices twice to remove draft records, the second time dowsing them with napalm and lighting them on fire. "The burning of paper, instead of children," Daniel wrote in explanation of their action, "when will you say no to this war?" Both brothers served time in prison for those break-ins but went on to engage in civil disobedience protests against later U.S. military interventions and the nuclear arms race.

After a lifetime of eloquent Christian activism, the Reverend William Sloan Coffin should be better known to Americans today.

Chaplain of Yale University during the Vietnam War, he spoke out strongly and early against the injustice of that incursion and went on to become president of SANE/FREEZE, the largest peace and justice organization in the United States, and minister of Riverside Church in Manhattan. The author of many powerful books, including *The Courage to Love* and *A Passion for the Possible*, he once said in an interview:

> I wonder if we Americans don't also have something that we should contribute, as it were, to the burial grounds of the world, something that would make the world a safer place. I think there is something in us. It is an attitude more than an idea. It lives less in the American mind than under the American skin. That is the notion that we are not only the most powerful nation in the world, which we certainly are, but that we are also the most virtuous. I think this pride is our bane and I think it is so deep-seated that it is going to take the sword of Christ's truth to do the surgical operation.

He also presciently said, "No nation, ours or any other, is well served by illusions of righteousness. All nations make decisions based on self-interest and then defend them in the name of morality."

Although Martin Luther King Jr. is well known, he is often viewed as an isolated icon on a moral pedestal rather than as one grand wave in an ocean of black prophetic Christians who constitute the long tradition that gave birth to him. There is David Walker, the free-born antislavery protester, who in 1829 published his famous *Appeal*, a blistering call for justice in which, as a devout Christian, he writes:

> I call upon the professing Christians, I call upon the philanthropist, I call upon the very tyrant himself, to show me a page of history, either sacred or profane, on which a verse can be found, which maintains, that the Egyptians heaped the *insupportable insult* upon the children of Israel, by telling them that they were not of the *human family*. Can the whites deny this charge? Have they not, after having reduced us to the deplorable condition of slaves under the feet, held us up as descending originally from the tribes of Monkeys or Orang-Outangs? O! my God! I appeal to every man of feeling—is not this insupportable? Is it not heaping the most gross insult upon our miseries, because they have got us under their feet and we cannot help ourselves? Oh! Pity us we pray thee, Lord Jesus, Master.

There is the deeply religious Ida B. Wells-Barnett, the anti-lynching activist who wrote shockingly of the gruesome truths of that peculiarly American form of terrorism in her pamphlet *A Red Record*, and who went on to found the women's club movement, the first civic activist organization for African American women. More Americans should remember Benjamin E. Mays. Ordained into the Baptist ministry, he served as the dean of the School of Religion at

Howard University and held the presidency of Morehouse College for twenty-five years, where he inspired Martin Luther King Jr. Mays helped launch the civil rights movement by participating in sit-ins in restaurants in Atlanta and was a leader in the fight against segregated education. There is the towering theologian Howard Thurman, also ordained into the Baptist ministry, dean of Rankin Chapel at Howard University and pastor of the first major U.S. interracial congregation in San Francisco, who traveled to India and met with Mahatma Gandhi and whose book *Jesus and the Disinherited* provided some of the philosophical foundation for the nonviolent civil rights movement.

The righteous fervor of this black prophetic Christian tradition is rich with ironies. When African slaves creatively appropriated the Christian movement under circumstances in which it was illegal to read, write, or worship freely, the schizophrenia of American Christianity was intensified. Some prophetic white Christians became founders of the abolitionist movement in partnership with ex-slaves, while other white Christians resorted to a Constantinian justification of the perpetuation of slavery. One's stand on slavery became a crucial litmus test to measure prophetic and Constantinian Christianity in America. The sad fact is that on this most glaring hypocrisy within American Christianity and democracy, most white Christians—and their beloved churches—were colossal failures based on prophetic criteria.

The vast majority of white American Christians supported the evil of slavery—and they did so often in the name of Jesus. When Abraham Lincoln declared in his profound Second Inaugural Address that both sides in the Civil War prayed to the same God—

"Neither party expected for the war, the magnitude, or the dura-
tion, which it has already attained. . . . Both read the same Bible,
and pray to the same God; and each invokes His aid against the
other"—he captured the horrible irony of this religious schizophrenia for the nation.

Black prophetic Christians—from Frederick Douglass to Martin
Luther King Jr.—have eloquently reminded us of the radical fis-
sure between prophetic and Constantinian Christianity, and King's
stirring Christian conviction and prophetic rhetoric fueled the democratizing movement that at last confronted the insidious in-
transigence of the color line. In fact, much of prophetic Christianity
in America stems from the prophetic black church tradition. The
Socratic questioning of the dogma of white supremacy, the
prophetic witness of love and justice, and the hard-earned hope
that sustains long-term commitment to the freedom struggle are
the rich legacy of the prophetic black church. Yet Constantinian
Christianity is so forceful that it is even making inroads into this
fervent black prophetic Christianity. The sad truth is that the black
church is losing its prophetic fervor in the age of the American
empire. The power of the Constantinian Christian coalition must
not be underestimated.

The rewards and respectability of the American empire that
tempt Christians of all colors cannot be overlooked. The free-
market fundamentalism that makes an idol of money and a fetish
of wealth seduces too many Christians. And when the major example of prophetic Christianity—the black church tradition—suc-
cumbs to this temptation and seduction, the very future of

American democracy is in peril. The crisis of Christian identity in America is central to democracy matters.

The separation of church and state is a pillar for any genuine democratic regime. All non-Christian citizens must have the same rights and liberties under the law as Christian citizens. But religion will always play a fundamental role in the shaping of the culture and politics in a democracy. All citizens must be free to speak out of their respective traditions with a sense of tolerance—and even respect—for other traditions. And in a society where Christians are the vast majority, we Christians must never promote a tyranny of this majority over an outnumbered minority in the name of Jesus. Ironically, Jesus was persecuted by a tyrannical majority (Roman imperial rulers in alliance with subjugated Jewish elites) as a prophetic threat to the status quo. Are not our nihilistic imperial rulers and their Constantinian Christian followers leading us on a similar path—the suffocating of prophetic voices and viewpoints that challenge their status quo?

The battle against Constantinianism cannot be won without a reempowerment of the prophetic Christian movement, because the political might and rhetorical fervor of the Constantinians are too threatening; a purely secular fight won't be won. As my Princeton colleague Jeffrey Stout has argued in his magisterial book *Democracy and Tradition* (2003), in order to make the world safe for King's legacy and reinvigorate the democratic tradition, we must question not only the dogmatic assumptions of the Constantinians but also those of many secular liberals who would banish religious discourse entirely from the public square and admonish disillu-

sioned prophetic Christians not to allow their voices and viewpoints to spill over into the public square. The liberalism of influential philosopher John Rawls and the secularism of philosopher
Richard Rorty—the major influences prevailing today in our courts
and law schools—are so fearful of Christian tainting that they call
for only secular public discourse on democracy matters. This radical secularism puts up a wall to prevent religious language in the
public square, to police religious-based arguments and permit only
secular ones. They see religious strife leading to social chaos and
authoritarianism.

For John Rawls, religious language in public discourse is divisive and dangerous. It deploys claims of religious faith that can
never be settled by appeals to reason. It fuels disagreements that
can never be overcome by rational persuasion. So he calls for a
public dialogue on fundamental issues that limits our appeals to
constitutional and civic ideals that cut across religious and secular
Americans and unite us in our loyalty to American democratic
practices. There is great wisdom in his proposal but it fails to acknowledge how our loyalty to constitutional and civic ideals may
have religious motivations. For prophetic Christians like Martin
Luther King Jr., his appeal to democratic ideals was grounded in his
Christian convictions. Should he—or we—remain silent about these
convictions when we argue for our political views? Does not personal integrity require that we put our cards on the table when we
argue for a more free and democratic America? In this way, Rawls's
fear of religion—given its ugly past in dividing citizens—asks the
impossible of us. Yet his concern is a crucial warning.

For Richard Rorty religious appeals are a conversation stopper.

They trump critical dialogue. They foreclose political debate. He wants to do away with any appeal to God in public life, especially since most appeals to God fuel the religious Right. He is a full-fledged secularist who sees little or no common good or public interest in the role of religion in civic discourse. Like Rawls, he supports the rights and liberties of religious citizens, but he wants to limit their public language to secular terms like democracy, equality, and liberty. His secular vision is motivated by a deep fear of the dogmatism and authoritarianism of the religious Right. There is much to learn from his view and many of his fears are warranted. But his secular policing of public life is too rigid and his secular faith is too pure. Ought we not to be concerned with the forms of dogmatism and authoritarianism in secular garb that trump dialogue and foreclose debate? Democratic practices—dialogue and debate in public discourse—are always messy and impure. And secular policing can be as arrogant and coercive as religious policing.

Prominent religious thinkers have also made impassioned arguments for the distancing of religion from American public discourse. Theologian Stanley Hauerwas's prophetic ecclesiasticism and John Milbank's radical orthodoxy—the major influences in seminaries and divinity schools—are so fearful of the tainting of the American empire that they call for a religious flight from the public square. For Hauerwas, Christians should be "resident aliens" in a corrupt American empire whose secular public discourse is but a thin cover for its robust nihilism. His aim is to preserve the integrity of the prophetic church by exposing the idolatry of Constantinian Christianity and bearing witness to the gospel of love and peace. His deep commitment to a prophetic church of compassion and pacifism in a world of cruelty and violence leads him to reject the secular policing of Rawls and Rorty and to high-light the captivity of Constantinian Christians to imperial America. But he finds solace only in a prophetic ecclesiastical refuge that prefigures the coming kingdom of God. His prophetic sensibilities resonate with me and I agree with his critique of Constantinian Christianity and imperial America. Yet he unduly downplays the prophetic Christian commitment to justice and our role as citizens to make America more free and democratic. For him, the pursuit of social justice is a bad idea for Christians because it lures them toward the idols of secular discourse and robs them of their dis-tinctive Christian identity. My defense of King's legacy requires that we accent justice as a Christian ideal and become even more active as citizens to change America without succumbing to secu-lar idols or imperial fetishes. To be a prophetic Christian is not to be against the world in the name of church purity; it is to be in the world but not of the world's nihilism, in the name of a loving Christ who proclaims the this-worldly justice of a kingdom to come.

Hauerwas's radical imperative of world-denial motivates Mil-bank's popular Christian orthodoxy that pits the culprits of com-modification and secularism against Christian socialism. His sophisticated wholesale attack on secular liberalism and modern capitalism is a fresh reminder of just how marginal prophetic Christianity has become in the age of the American empire. But, like Hauerwas, he fails to appreciate the moral progress, political breakthroughs, and spiritual freedoms forged by the heroic efforts of modern citizens of religious and secular traditions. It is just as dangerous to overlook the gains of modernity procured by prophetic religious and progressive secular citizens as it is to overlook the blindness of Constantinian Christians and imperial secularists. And these gains cannot be preserved and deepened by reverting to ecclesiastical refuges or sectarian orthodoxies. Instead they require candor about our religious integrity and democratic identity that leads us to critique and resist Constantinian Christianity and imperial America.

All four towering figures—Rawls, Rorty, Hauerwas, and Milbank—have much to teach us and are forces for good in many ways. Yet they preclude a robust democratic Christian identity that builds on the legacy of prophetic Christian-led social movements. Jeffrey Stout—himself the most religiously musical, theologically learned, and philosophically subtle of all secular writers in America today— has, by contrast, argued that American democrats must join forces with the legacy of Christian protest exemplified by Martin Luther King Jr. He knows that the future of the American democratic experiment may depend on revitalizing this legacy. The legacies of prophetic Christianity put a premium on the kind of human being one chooses to be rather than the amount of commodities one possesses. They thereby constitute a wholesale onslaught against nihilism—in all of its forms—and strike a blow for decency and integrity. They marshal religious energies for democratic aims, yet are suspicious of all forms of idolatry, including democracy itself as an idol. They preserve their Christian identity and its democratic commitments, without coercing others and conflating church and state spheres.

There can be a new democratic Christian identity in America

only if imperial realities are acknowledged and prophetic legacies are revitalized. And despite the enormous resources of imperial elites to fan and fuel Constantinian Christianity, the underfunded and unpopular efforts of democrats and prophetic Christians must become more visible and vocal. The organizations of prophetic Christianity, such as the World Council of Churches, the civic action group Sojourners, and the black prophetic churches, must fight their way back into prominence in our public discourse. They must recognize that they have been under a kind of siege by the Constantinians and have not lost their dominance by accident.

Ironically, the powerful political presence of imperial Christians today is inspired by the success of the democratic Christian-led movement of Martin Luther King Jr. The worldly engagement of King's civil rights movement encouraged Constantinian Christians to become more organized and to partner with the power elites of the American empire. The politicization of Christian fundamentalism was a direct response to King's prophetic Christian legacy. It began as a white backlash against King's heritage in American public life, and it has always had a racist undercurrent—as with Bob Jones University, which until recently barred interracial dating.

The rise of Constantinian Christianity in America went hand in hand with the Republican Party's realignment of American politics—with their use of racially coded issues (busing, crime, affirmative action, welfare) to appeal to southern conservatives and urban white centrists. This political shift coincided with appeals to influential Jewish neoconservatives primarily concerned with the fragile security and international isolation of the state of Israel. In particular, the sense of Jewish desperation during the Yom Kippur War of 1973—fully understandable given the threat of Jewish annihilation only thirty years after the vicious holocaust in Europe—drove the unholy alliance of American Republicans, Christian evangelicals, and Jewish neoconservatives.

On the domestic front, the fierce battle over admissions and employment slots produced a formidable backlash led by Jewish neoconservatives and white conservatives against affirmative action. The right-wing coalition of Constantinian Christians and Jewish neoconservatives helped elect Ronald Reagan in 1980. The fact that 35 percent of the most liberal nonwhite group—American Jews—voted for Reagan was a prescient sign of what was to come. When the Reverend Jerry Falwell of the Moral Majority received the Jabotinsky Award in 1981 in Israel, Constantinian Christianity had arrived on the international stage, with Jewish conservatism as its supporter. Imperial elites—including corporate ones with huge financial resources—here and abroad recognized just how useful organized Constantinian Christians could be for their nihilistic aims.

The rise of Constantinian Christian power in our democracy has progressed in stages. First, ecumenical groups like the World Council of Churches, the National Council of Churches, and liberal mainline denominations (Episcopalians, Presbyterians, Lutherans, and Congregationalists)—who spoke out in defense of the rights of people of color, workers, women, gays, and lesbians—were targeted. The Christian fundamentalists (with big money behind them) lashed out with vicious attacks against the prophetic Christian voices, who were branded "liberal," and worked to discredit the voices of moderation. In McCarthyist fashion, they equated the liberation theology movement, which put a limelight on the plight of the poor, with Soviet Communism. They cast liberal seminaries (especially my beloved Union Theological Seminary in New York City) as sinful havens of freaks, gays, lesbians, black radicals, and guilty white wimps. Such slanderous tactics have largely cowed the Christian Left, nearly erasing it off the public map.

The Christian fundamentalists have also tried to recruit Constantinian Christians of color in order to present a more diverse menagerie of faces to the imperial elites in the White House, Congress, state houses, and city halls, and on TV. The manipulative elites of the movement knew that this integrated alliance would attract even more financial support from big business to sustain a grassroots organizing campaign in imperial churches across the country. The veneer of diversity is required for the legitimacy of imperial rule today.

The last stage in the rise of the Constantinians was their consolidation of power by throwing their weight around with well-organized political action groups, most notably the Christian Coalition and the Moral Majority. With this political coordination they gained clout, power, legitimacy, and respectability within the golden gates of the American empire—they were acknowledged as mighty movers, shakers, and brokers who had to be reckoned with in the private meetings of the plutocrats and their politicians. Imperial elites recognized just how useful the Constantinian Christians could be for their nihilistic aims. The journey for Constantinian Christians from Ronald Reagan's election in 1980 to

George W. Bush's selection in 2000 has been a roaring success—based on the world's nihilistic standards.

Never before in the history of the American Republic has a group of organized Christians risen to such prominence in the American empire. And this worldly success—a bit odd for a fundamentalist group with such otherworldly aspirations—has sent huge ripples across American Christendom. Power, might, size, status, and material possessions—all paraphernalia of the nihilism of the American empire—became major themes of American Christianity. It now sometimes seems that all Christians speak in one voice when in fact it is only that the loudness of the Constantinian element of American Christianity has so totally drowned out the prophetic voices. Imperial Christianity, market spirituality, money-obsessed churches, gospels of prosperity, prayers of let's-make-a-deal with God or help me turn my wheel of fortune have become the prevailing voice of American Christianity. In this version of Christianity the precious blood at the foot of the cross becomes mere Kool-Aid to refresh eager upwardly mobile aspirants in the nihilistic American game of power and might. And there is hardly a mumbling word heard about social justice, resistance to institutional evil, or courage to confront the powers that be—with the glaring exception of abortion.

Needless to say, the commodification of Christianity is an old phenomenon—and a central one in American life past and present. Yet the frightening scope and depth of this commercialization of Christianity is new. There is no doubt that the churches reflect and refract the larger market-driven nihilism of our society and world.

Yet it is the nearly wholesale eclipse of nonmarket values and visions—of love, justice, compassion, and kindness to strangers—that is terrifying. Where are the Christian voices outraged at the greed of corporate elites while millions of children live in poverty? Do American Christians even know that the three richest men in the world have more wealth than the combined gross domestic product of the bottom forty-eight countries or that the personal wealth of the 225 richest individuals is equal to the annual income of the poorest 47 percent of the entire world's population? Philanthropy is fine, but what of justice, institutional fairness, and structural accountability?

There are, however, groups of prophetic Christians who are taking up the challenge of confronting the rise of the Christian Right and have realized the necessity of countering those powerful organizations with their own. There is Jim Wallis, who leads the activist group Sojourners; the Reverend James Forbes of Riverside Church in New York City; Sujay Johnson Cork of the Hampton Preachers' Conference; the Reverend Charles Adams of Hartford Memorial Church in Detroit; the Reverend Jeremiah Wright of Trinity Church in Chicago; Bishop Charles E. Blake of West Angeles Church of God in Christ; the Reverend J. Alfred Smith of Allen Temple in Oakland; and Father Michael Pfleger of Faith Community of Saint Sabina in Chicago. And there are quite a few more.

Yet it is undeniable that the challenge of keeping the prophetic Christian movement vital and vibrant in the age of the American empire is largely unmet as of yet. The pervasive sleepwalking in American churches in regard to social justice is frightening. The movement led by Martin Luther King Jr.—the legacy of which has been hijacked by imperial Christians—forged the most subtle and significant democratic Christian identity of modern times. And it now lies in ruins. Can prophetic Christians make its dry bones live again?

The Constantinian Christianity of the Bush administration— especially of President Bush, Attorney General John Ashcroft, and Congressman Tom DeLay—whatever authentic pietistic dimensions it may have, must not be the model of American Christian identity. Its nihilistic policies and quests for power and might supersede any personal confessions of humility and compassion. Even the most seemingly pious can inflict great harm. Constantine himself flouted his piety even as he continued to dominate and conquer peoples. Yet a purely secular effort against the religious zealotry will never be powerful enough to prevail; it is only with a coalition of the prophetic Christians of all colors, the prophetic Jews and Muslims and Buddhists, and the democratic secularists that we can preserve the American democratic experiment.

The recent controversy over Mel Gibson's *The Passion of the Christ* reveals the nihilistic undercurrents of the conservative coalition and potential rifts within it. The vicious Christian anti-Judaism and anti-Semitism over the past eighteen centuries stem primarily from the wedding of biblical narratives of Jesus's Crucifixion that highlight Jewish responsibility and Roman innocence to Constantine's incorporation of Christianity into imperial power. As long as the early Christians—themselves largely Jewish— were a persecuted minority in the Roman empire, their biblical claims about Jewish culpability and Roman indifference regarding the murder of Jesus were a relatively harmless intra-Jewish debate in the first century AD about a prophetic Jew who challenged the Jewish colonial elites and Roman imperial authorities. For example, when the phrase "the Jews" is used sixteen times in Mark, Luke, and Matthew and seventy-one times in John, these writers of the synoptic Gospels—themselves Jews—were engaged in an intramural debate between themselves and non-Christian Jews. Both groups were persecuted by imperial Roman authorities. And all knew of the thuggery of such authorities—including that of Pontius Pilate fifty years before. With the Roman destruction of the Jewish temple in AD 70, rabbinical Judaism emerged alongside the Jewish-led Christian movement. The Christian and Judaic struggle for the souls of Jews in imperial Rome was intense, yet under oppressive conditions for both groups.

With the adoption of Christianity as the official religion of the Roman empire in the fourth century AD—and the persecution of all other religions—the intramural debate became lethal. And the phrase "the Jews" in the Gospels became the basis of a vicious Christian anti-Judaism and pernicious imperial policy that blamed, attacked, maimed, and murdered Jews of Judaic faith. With the injection of race, Christian anti-Judaism (a religious bigotry) became Christian anti-Semitism (a racist bigotry). Jews who converted to Christianity could avoid the former, but all Jews suffered the latter. And the history of both bigotries is a crime against humanity—then and now.

Mel Gibson's gory film of Jesus's murder, which verges on a pornography of violence, resonates deeply with the ignorance and innocence of sincere Constantinian Christians in the American empire, whose grasp of the source of anti-Semitism is weak and whose complicity with imperial arrogance is ignored. His portrayal of Jewish responsibility and Roman innocence fits the centuries-long pattern of Christian anti-Semitism—in its effect, not in his intention.

Ironically, those Jews who eagerly aligned themselves with Constantinian Christians to defend imperial America and the colonial policies of the Israeli state now see the deep anti-Semitism of their Christian fundamentalist allies. And they are right. But these same Jewish conservatives—Constantinian Jews—fail to see their own complicity with imperial American elites who support and condone colonial policies and racist anti-Arab sentiments of Israeli conservative elites. Democracy matters—promoted by prophetic Christians, Jews, Muslims, Buddhists, and secular progressives—require moral consistency and ethical integrity. We all fall short yet we must never fail to fight all forms of bigotry, especially when racist propaganda is conjoined to nihilistic quests for power and might. Will the deep dimensions of Christian anti-Semitism shatter the conservative coalition in imperial America? Will Jewish elites in Hollywood begin to question the racist stereotypes of other groups they've condoned now that this controversy has turned against them?

I speak as a Christian—one whose commitment to democracy is very deep but whose Christian convictions are even deeper. Democracy is not my faith. And American democracy is not my idol. To see the Gospel of Jesus Christ bastardized by imperial Christians and pulverized by Constantinian believers and then exploited by nihilistic elites of the American empire makes my blood boil. To be a Christian—a follower of Jesus Christ—is to love wisdom, love justice, and love freedom. This is the radical love in Christian freedom and the radical freedom in Christian love that embraces Socratic questioning, prophetic witness, and tragicomic hope. If Christians do not exemplify this love and freedom, then we side with the nihilists of the Roman empire (cowardly elite Romans and subjugated Jews) who put Jesus to a humiliating death. Instead of receiving his love in freedom as a life-enhancing gift of grace, we end up believing in the idols of the empire that nailed him to the cross. I do not want to be numbered among those who sold their souls for a mess of pottage—who surrendered their democratic Christian identity for a comfortable place at the table of the American empire while, like Lazarus, the least of these cried out and I was too intoxicated with worldly power and might to hear, beckon, and heed their cries. To be a Christian is to live dangerously, honestly, freely—to step in the name of love as if you may land on nothing, yet to keep stepping because the something that sustains you no empire can give you and no empire can take away. This is the kind of vision and courage required to enable the renewal of prophetic, democratic Christian identity in the age of the American empire.

6

THE NECESSARY ENGAGEMENT
WITH YOUTH CULTURE

It is a fallacy of radical youth to demand all or nothing, and to view every partial activity as compromise. Either engage in something that will bring revolution and transformation all at one blow, or do nothing, it seems to say. But compromise is really only a desperate attempt to reconcile the irreconcilable. It is not compromise to study to understand the world in which one lives, to seek expression for one's inner life, to work to harmonize it and make it an integer, nor is it compromise to work in some small sphere for the harmonization of social life and the relations between men who work together, a harmonization that will bring democracy into every sphere of life.

—RANDOLPH S. BOURNE,
Youth and Life (1913)

When Public Enemy first came out we used to say "Public Enemy, we're agents for the preservation of the Black mind. We're media hijackers." We worked to hijack the media and put it in our own form. . . . Every time we checked for ourselves on the news they were locking us up anyway, so the interpretation coming from Rap was a lot clearer. That's why I call Rap the Black CNN.

Rap is now a worldwide phenomenon. Rap is the CNN for young people all over the world.

—CHUCK D with YUSUF JAH,

Fight the Power: Rap, Race, and Reality (1997)

When we ask, what is the state of Hiphop?, the quick answer is that Hiphop (the community) must mature to a level of self-government where it creates, regulates, and profits from its own elements, resources, and intellectual properties. The state of Hiphop is that Hiphop is being negatively exploited by the recording industries of America who manipulate its public image to sell the fantasy of pimpin', thuggin', hoein', flashin', flossin', and ballin' to predominantly young White Rap fans that are impressed by such behaviors. On the one hand it is Hiphop's rebellious image that attracts young people to it. However, on the other hand, the real lives of those that live around pimps, thugs, whores, drug dealers, etc., are far from being just fantasies of defiance that you can turn off and on when you want to feel sexy or macho! The real lives of those that are affected by injustice, lawlessness, and corruption created (and continue to create) Hiphop as a way out of oppression.

—KRS-ONE, *Ruminations* (2003)

In past moments of national division, young people have played a disproportionate role in deepening the American democratic experiment. The black freedom struggle and the anti-war movement in the 1960s were largely sustained owing to their vision and courage. As older folk become jaded, disillusioned, and weary, the lively moral energy of reflective and compassionate young people can play a vital role in pushing democratic momen-

tum. Yet one of the most effective strategies of corporate marke-
teers has been to target the youth market with distractive amusement and saturate them with pleasurable sedatives that steer them
away from engagement with issues of peace and justice. The inces-
sant media bombardment of images (of salacious bodies and mindless violence) on TV and in movies and music convinces many
young people that the culture of gratification—a quest for insatiable
pleasure, endless titillation, and sexual stimulation—is the only
way of being human. Hedonistic values and narcissistic identities
produce emotionally stunted young people unable to grow up and
unwilling to be responsible democratic citizens. The market-
driven media lead many young people to think that life is basically
about material toys and social status. Democratic ideas of making
the world more just, or striving to be a decent and compassionate
person, are easily lost or overlooked.

This media bombardment not only robs young people of their
right to struggle for maturity—by glamorizing possessive individualism at the expense of democratic individuality—but also leaves
them ill equipped to deal with the spiritual malnutrition that awaits
them after their endless pursuit of pleasure. This sense of emptiness of the soul holds for wealthy kids in the vanilla suburbs and
poor kids in the chocolate cities. Neither the possession of commodities nor the fetishizing of commodities satisfies young people's need for love and self-confidence. Instead we witness
personal depression, psychic pain, and individual loneliness fueling media-influenced modes of escapism. These include the high
use of drugs like cocaine and Ecstasy; the growing popularity of
performing sex acts at incredibly young ages, such as middle-

school-age girls giving boys blow jobs because it will make them "cool"; and the way in which so many kids have become addicted to going online and instant messaging or creating Weblogs in which they assume an alternate personality. This disgraceful numbing of the senses, dulling of the mind, and confining of life to an eternal present—with a lack of connection to the past and no vision for a different future—is an insidious form of soul murder. And we wonder why depression escalates and suicides increase among our precious children.

The most dangerous mode of dealing with this bombardment is addiction—to drugs, alcohol, sex, or narrow forms of popularity or success. These addictions leave little room or time for democratic efforts to become mature, concerned about others, or politically engaged in social change. The popular way of escaping from the pain and emptiness is self-medication—the first step toward self-violation and self-destruction. This is why so many—too many—of the youth of America are drifting, rootless, deracinated, and denuded. They have hardly a sense of their history, little grasp of what shapes them, and no vital vision of their human potential. Many have been reduced to a bundle of desires targeted by corporate America for consumption. Their armor of life is often too feeble to enable them to withstand the emotional trauma generated, in part, by the fast-paced capitalist culture of consumption that confronts them. In short, many lack the necessary navigational skills to cope with the challenges and crises in life—disappointment, disease, death. This is why so many are enacting the nihilism of meaninglessness and hopelessness in their lives that mirrors the nihilism of the adult world—often they are so disillusioned in large part because they can see that the adult world itself is so bereft of morality.

Yet some young folk do persevere and prevail: those who are dissatisfied with mere material toys and illusions of security. They hunger for something more, thirst for something deeper. They want caring attention, wise guidance, and compassionate counsel. They desire democratic individuality, community, and society. They know something is wrong with America and something is missing in their lives. They long for energizing visions worthy of pursuit and sacrifice that will situate their emaciated souls in a story bigger than themselves and locate their inflated egos (that only conceal deep insecurities and anxieties) in a narrative grander than themselves. Their emaciated souls contain a rage that often strikes out at the world; their inflated egos yield a cocky pose and posture that defies authority, whether legitimate or illegitimate. A grand story and a large narrative—especially democratic ones—can channel their longings into mature efforts to contribute in a mean-ingful way to making the world a better place. This longing is the raw stuff of democracy matters.

Like every younger generation, our kids today see clearly the hypocrisies and mendacities of our society, and as they grow up they begin to question in a fundamental way some of the lies that they've received from society. They also begin to see that their ed-ucation has been distorted and sugarcoated and has sidestepped so many uncomfortable truths. This often leads to an ardent disap-pointment, and even anger, about the failures of our society to con-sistently uphold the democratic and humanitarian values that can be born in youths in this phase of their life. This new sense of conscience in young people is a profound force that adult society should take much more seriously. In fact, we should understand the expressions of this moral outrage as having a profound kind of wisdom, even as we must also help to channel that outrage into a more productive sense of commitment to find a positive way forward.

In the political sphere, the most significant expression today of this mix of anger, disappointment, and yet a tough-edged longing is the democratic globalization movement here and abroad. Although still in the early stages, this movement to establish democratic accountability of the American empire and its global corporate behemoths is disproportionately led by the youth culture. The historical day of protest—February 15, 2003—in which millions of people in over six hundred cities (including nearly two hundred U.S. cities) protested the likelihood of a U.S. violation of international law in its invasion of Iraq exemplifies the deep democratic energy and moral fervor that youth can bring to bear. Other protests in Seattle, Prague, Washington, Rome, and Davos, Switzerland— driven largely by young people—focused international attention on the antidemocratic character of global world power centers that reinforce American imperial rule.

The central thrust of this movement is criticism of the dogma of free-market fundamentalism and the increasing wealth inequality all around the world that the slavish devotion to the dogma has produced. The movement also targets the aggressive militarism of the U.S. government and the escalating authoritarianism here and around the world. The impressive efforts to create lasting institutions out of the energy of these protests—such as the public-interest groups MoveOn and Global Citizens Campaign—exemplify democratic commitment in action. Much of the support for and enthusiasm generated by these organizations is owing to youth culture. One of the tasks to which I am devoted—as a democratic intellectual of middle age!—is to help make this movement more multiracial by linking it to black youth culture. One way I've worked at doing this is by engaging with the profound power and energy of hip-hop culture and rap music, by taking it as seriously as it should be taken.

Although hip-hop culture has become tainted by the very excesses and amorality it was born in rage against, the best of rap music and hip-hop culture still expresses stronger and more clearly than any cultural expression in the past generation a profound indictment of the moral decadence of our dominant society. An unprecedented cultural breakthrough created by talented poor black youths in the hoods of the empire's chocolate cities, hip-hop has by now transformed the entertainment industry and culture here and around the world. The fundamental irony of hip-hop is that it has become viewed as a nihilistic, macho, violent, and bling-bling phenomenon when in fact its originating impulse was a fierce disgust with the hypocrisies of adult culture—disgust with the selfishness, capitalist callousness, and xenophobia of the culture of adults, both within the hood and in the society at large. For example, the most popular hip-hop artists today are Outkast from Atlanta, Georgia. On their first album over a decade ago, in "True Dat," Ruben Bailey explained their name—an explanation that goes back to the original roots of hip-hop:

Operatin' under the crooked American system too long, Outkast, pronounced outcast, adjective meaning homeless or unaccepted in society, but let's dig deeper than that.

Are you an outcast? If you understand the basic principles and fundamental truths continued within this music you probably are. If you think it's all about pimpin' hoes and slammin Cadillac doors you probably a cracker, or a nigga that think he a cracker, or maybe just don't understand.

An outcast is someone who is not considered to be part of the normal world. He's looked at differently. He's not accepted because of his clothes, his hair, his occupation, his beliefs or his skin color. Now look at yourself, are you an outcast? I know I am, as a matter of fact, fuck bein' anything else.

The first stages of hip-hop were hot. Coming from the margins of society, the lyrics and rhythms of Grandmaster Flash and the Furious Five, Kool Herc, Rakim, Paris, the Poor Righteous Teachers, Afrikaa Bambaataa, and, above all, KRS-ONE and Public Enemy (led by Chuck D) unleashed incredible democratic energies. Their truth telling about black suffering and resistance in America was powerful. The political giants of hip-hop all expressed and continue to express the underground outlook of Outkast: righteous indignation at the dogmas and nihilism of imperial America.

Yet hip-hop was soon incorporated into the young American mainstream and diluted of its prophetic fervor.

With the advent of the giants of the next phase—Tupac Shakur, Ice-T, Ice Cube, Biggie Smalls, and Snoop Dogg—linguistic genius and gangster sentiments began to be intertwined. Ironically, their artistic honesty revealed subversive energy and street prowess in their work and life. As the entertainment industry began to mainstream the music, that street prowess became dominant—with the racist stereotypes of black men as hypercriminal and hypersexual and black women as willing objects of their conquests. The companies perceived that white kids were much more interested in the more violence-ridden, misogynist mode than in the critical, prophetic mode. This packaging for eager rebellious youth in vanilla suburbs—now 72 percent of those who buy hip-hop CDs and even more who illegally download them—led to an economic boom for the industry, until its recent downturn. Black Star, the progressive duo of Mos Def and Talib Kweli, responded to this market focus exclusively on the bottom line this way in "Hater Players":

> We started to see cats shouting "player hater" to anyone who had nerve to critique they wack shit. A lot of rich players are making wack ass music, that's the bottom line! I remember when the worst thing you could be was a sell out. Then the sell-outs starting running things. We call this song "Hater Players" because there are many players who hate the fact that we do this for love.

The prophetic Lauryn Hill notes in "Lost Ones":

> It's funny how money change a situation
> Miscommunication lead to complication
> My emancipation don't fit your equation
> I was on the humble you on every station

It is important not to confuse prophetic hip-hop with Constantinian hip-hop. Prophetic hip-hop remains true to the righteous indignation and political resistance of deep democratic energies. Constantinian hip-hop defers to the dogmas and nihilisms of imperial America. As DA Smart says in "Where Ya At?":

> What you trying to pull eatin' us like cannibals
> Whatever happened to that forty acres and that
>   animal
> Now you tryin to use integration just to fool us
> Like Malcolm said we been hoodwinked and
>   bamboozled.

That such powerful poetry and insightful social critiques could be created by youths who have been flagrantly disregarded, demeaned, and demonized by the dominant market-driven culture—targeted as cannon fodder by a racist criminal-justice system and a growing prison-industrial complex, in disgraceful schools and shattered families (including too many irresponsible, unemployed fathers) and violent environments—is a remarkable testament to the vital perspective and energy that can be injected into our democracy by the young, who have not made their compromises yet with the corrupted system.

What a horrible irony it is that this poetry and critique could be co-opted by the consumer preferences of suburban white youths—white youths who long for rebellious energy and exotic amusement in their own hollow bourgeois world. But the black voices from the hood were the most genuine, authentic voices from outside the flaccid mainstream market culture that they could find. So the recording and fashion industries seized on this market opportunity. The present state of hip-hop—with great talents like Jay-Z, Eminem, Dr. Dre, Master P, Kanye West, Pharrell, Killer Mike, Dead Prez, and, above all, Outkast—is tenuous. Although it remains a major force in the industry, much of the talent has gone underground. And as Imani Perry shows in her superb book, *Prophets of the Hood* (2004), the future of hip-hop is local music. Meanwhile the neo-soul movement—Jill Scott, The Roots, Kindred, Anthony Hamilton, Ruff Endz, Dru Hill, Donnie, India.Arie, Alicia Keys—is a mellowing out of the roughness and toughness. Just as is the revival of the perennial genius of Gerald Levert, Aretha Franklin, Teddy Pendergrass, Stevie Wonder, Luther Vandross, Ronald Isley, and R. Kelly. Yet more underground hip-hop may surface soon. I hope so—for the sake of democratic energies in American life—because hip-hop has made such vital contributions to not only national but international political truth telling.

Like the forms of black music in the past, hip-hop seized the imaginations of young people across the globe. Prophetic hip-hop has told painful truths about their internal struggles and how the decrepit schools, inadequate health care, unemployment, and drug markets of the urban centers of the American empire have wounded their souls. Yet Constantinian hip-hop revels in the fetishism of commodities, celebrates the materialism, hedonism, and narcissism of the culture (the bling! bling!) and promotes a degrading of women, gays, lesbians, and gangster enemies. In short, hip-hop is a full-scale mirror of the best and worst, the virtuous and vicious, aspects of our society and world.

Hip-hop culture and rap music are, in many ways, an indictment of the old generation even as they imitate and emulate us in a raw and coarse manner. The defiant and insightful voices of this new generation lyrically proclaim that they have been relatively unloved, uncared for, and unattended to by adults too self-indulgent, too self-interested, and too self-medicated to give them the necessary love, care, and attention to flower and flourish. Only their beloved mothers—often overworked, underpaid, and wrestling with a paucity of genuine intimacy—are spared. They also indict the American empire for its mendacity and hypocrisy—not in a direct anti-imperialist language but in a poetic rendering of emotional deficits and educational defects resulting from the unequal institutional arrangements of the empire.

It is important that all democrats engage and encourage prophetic voices in hip-hop—voices that challenge youth to be self-critical rather than self-indulgent, Socratic rather than hedonistic. This is why I strongly support and participate in the efforts of Russell Simmons and Benjamin Chavis to organize hip-hop into a political force that accents the plight of youth. I also support the vision of KRS-ONE and others behind the Hip Hop Temple, which teaches youth the prophetic aims of underground hip-hop. There is also the organization of L. Londell Mcmillan—the Arts Empowerment Collective—which protects prophetic artists from abuse by the industry; and there are annual gatherings of the great musical genius Prince at Paisley Park, which bring the older generation together with the young artists in order to wrestle with political issues and enjoy performances. Prophetic hip-hop is precious soil in which the seeds of democratic individuality, community, and society can sprout.

I have experienced this sprouting on an intimate level in the making of my first CD, *Sketches of My Culture* (2001, Artemis), and my double CD, *Street Knowledge* (2004, Roc Diamond). The deep solidarity and community—shot through with critical exchange and political reflection—in Crystal Clear Studios in my old black neighborhood of Glen Elder, in Sacramento, California, is a vital democratic space for young people. Our group—Four Black Men Who Mean Business (4BMWMB)—brings together the inimitable producer and songwriter Derek "D.O.A." Allen, the initiator and songwriter Michael Dailey, the elder leader and songwriter Clifton West (my beloved blood brother), and myself. Our aim is to teach youths the prophetic history of black music and to reveal to them the political foundations of hip-hop. We build bridges between the older and younger generations by speaking directly to them and performing with them in their own idioms and styles. These CDs are danceable education for artistic and political ends. In this way, democracy matters are woven into hip-hop culture in a respectful yet critical manner.

Hip-hop culture is hardly the only vehicle for such outreach, though it is a vital one. The disaffection of so many youths stems in large part from their perception that the adult community neither understands nor cares about the issues in their lives. Even within the university world, where the highest calling should be to spark the fires of intellectual exploration and to prepare young minds for engaged and productive participation in our democracy, the mandates of the market have attained prominence. The narrow quest for success crowds out the noble effort to be great—greatness understood as using one's success to make the world a better place for all.

A market-driven technocratic culture has infiltrated university life, with the narrow pursuit of academic trophies and the business of generating income from grants and business partnerships taking precedence over the fundamental responsibility of nurturing young minds. It is imperative for the adults who have made the life of the mind their life's calling to be engaged with the wider community and play a vital role in furthering the national discourse on the important issues of the day by exercising the ways of truth telling that engage youth. Young people are acutely aware of the hypocrisies of so many adults in the political and business worlds, and that's why those of us in the universities who are free to speak more frankly without worries of recriminations—though the degree of that freedom is under fire—can create such an important bridge.

This is why I have made not only a serious commitment to teaching and writing in the academy but also a substantive conviction to communicate to the larger culture. I have taught in prisons for over twenty years. My numerous appearances on C-SPAN and other TV networks provide occasions to challenge fellow citizens on burning issues of the day. My weekly commentary on Tavis Smiley's National Public Radio show offers deep democratic viewpoints on U.S. foreign and domestic policies. My grappling with the legacy of slavery with young kids on Linda Ellerbee's *Nick News* highlights democratic progress. My cochairing of the National Parenting Association with Sylvia Ann Hewlett (including our books, *The War Against Parents* [1998] and *Taking Parenting Public* [2002]) spotlights the needs of children; and my recent role as Counselor West in the last two *Matrix* films supports the deep democratic vision of the Wachowskis. Furthermore, the annual Pass-the-Mic tour of several cities—with crowds of thousands paying $50 a ticket to engage in a discussion of serious issues—that I do with Tavis Smiley and Michael Eric Dyson (the towering public intellectual of his generation) joins older and younger people in a democratic space of critique and resistance to imperial America. I have also tried to support brilliant young democratic intellectuals like Eddie Glaude Jr. of Princeton University and Farah Jasmine Griffin of Columbia University. On each of these fronts, I have been amazed at the hunger of young people for the expression of democratic ideals and for critical conversation.

I am especially inspired in my own outreach by the example of Tavis Smiley, because he is the most influential democratic intellectual in mass media of the younger generation—and possibly of any generation. His vibrant presence in the culture is always accompanied by his relentless wrestling with race and empire. He has done more than anyone to educate and inspire young people, especially young black people, to attend to democracy matters. Tavis Smiley's commentaries appear twice a week on *The Tom Joyner Morning Show*—the black radio show with the largest audience in the country (twelve million people). His historic National Public Radio show and his TV talk show on public television are unprecedented: never in the history of mass media in America has anyone—of any color—had a National Public Radio show and a show on public television at the same time. His nine books sell swiftly. And both his Tavis Smiley Foundation for young leaders and his annual black think tank on C-SPAN are major forces for good. He understands and embodies the kind of vision and courage needed to make youth culture central to democracy matters.

I do not believe that the life of an academic—or at least all academics—should be narrowly contained within the university walls or made to serve narrow technocratic goals. Surely academics must delve deeply into the more specialized concerns of their chosen fields and must seek to make significant contributions to the furthering of those concerns—and I have done my share of writing articles that are narrowly focused on recondite issues in philosophy and specialized books such as *The American Evasion of Philosophy: A Genealogy of Pragmatism* (1989) and *Keeping Faith* (1993). But I also have always believed that there is a vital public role for those academics who are inclined to engage with the broiling issues of the day. The participation of academics in political protests and in the coalition building behind the most successful democratic social movements in our history has been so vital, often joining workers, students, disenfranchised citizens, activists, and politically engaged academics in potent protests of elite corruptions and bringing youths into that energized democratic fold. Indeed, it is out of an early embrace of this rich tradition of academic engagement in the democratic doings of society—which I admired so much in so many of the intellectuals prominent when I was coming up—that I have devoted myself so determinedly to taking part. But the technocratic management culture on the rise in our universities today offers few such democratic rewards— rather crude rebukes—for those academics who embark on projects that fall outside the narrow range of the technocratic vision, especially if those projects are politically provocative. This is the narrow-minded mentality that I ran into head-on in my all-too- notorious encounter with the president of Harvard, Lawrence Summers.

My rich and promising democratic experiences of weaving a web of interconnections between the academy, mass media, prisons, churches, and the street were called into question because they did not fit into the narrow field of his technocratic vision. For Summers, the role of the professor is to engage in an elite and comfortable pursuit of academic work that is pleasing to a market- driven university management and imperial America. His vision puts a premium on accumulating academic trophies and generating sizable income in the form of government contracts, foundation grants, and business partnerships that secure the prestige of the university. This technocratic view of the academy fences professors off from the larger democratic culture and has made university life too remote from that of the larger society that supports it. Summers found little or no value in my efforts to cultivate young minds in quality interactions outside the academy. To him, outreach to the public at large, and especially to youth culture, fell outside the mission of the university. Furthermore, he questioned my academic accomplishments and my political affiliations, without bothering either to read any of my work or to develop an understanding of how it has been regarded by the wider academic community. I would have preferred that the meeting between us that prompted me to resign from Harvard had never become public, but given that the press did have a field day with the story (full of both honest distortions and dishonest attacks), it is important for me to set the record straight. Only he and I know the truth—and the story is representative of a callous disregard for the vocation of democratically engaged intellectuals in too much of American academic life.

In early October 2001, shortly after Summers arrived on campus, I was summoned to meet with him. My friend and department head Henry Louis Gates Jr. had kindly put me on notice that President Lawrence Summers would like to talk to me. I had neither met President Summers nor would I have recognized him on the street. I had no idea what he looked like. I'd heard a few rumors about his bumpy start as leader of Harvard. He had reputedly made remarks about putting the famous Afro-American Studies Department in its place. He had held meetings with department heads and deliberately skipped over the Afro-American Studies head, Professor Gates. I had also heard that in a meeting with black employees he had said that the beneficial results of affirmative action were not yet convincing. And there was the story of his infamous memo at the World Bank in which he suggested transporting dangerous polluted material to sub-Saharan Africa because that region suffered from overpopulation. I took those rumors with a grain of salt, though, because I had seen little hard evidence that confirmed them. I was annoyed about some of the early signs of his administration—especially regarding opposition to a living-wage campaign I strongly supported. I had also been annoyed by the administration's request at the start of the term that I reduce my course on Afro-American studies from seven hundred to four hundred students because, it said, there was no room at Harvard to teach such a large class. The latter matter dragged on for three weeks as I refused to cut back on my class, until I finally settled for teaching all seven hundred students in the basement of a Catholic church off campus owing to the support of its prophetic priest.

Just prior to my date with President Summers, Professor Gates took me aside and showed me a three-page single-spaced letter he had written to the president reviewing my sixteen books and eight coedited works, and describing my faculty advisory roles with numerous student groups. I was taken aback to discover that I was apparently under scrutiny, and I couldn't believe the amount of energy and time Professor Gates had been required to devote to the task; it seemed unnecessary, even wasteful. As a University Professor at Harvard—a special kind of professorship that resides in no department or program—I was free to teach wherever I so desired and able to cut back on my teaching load if I so desired, though I had not at all desired to and had in fact added to mine.

I didn't think I should have needed such an introduction, or needed to justify myself, to the president.

When I entered his office, Professor Summers seemed nervous as he shook my hand; frankly, he seemed uneasy in his own skin. Then, to my astonishment, this man I'd never met before started our conversation by saying that he wanted me to help him f— up Professor Harvey Mansfield, a leading conservative professor who has openly disparaged the sizable presence of black students and women at Harvard. President Summers apparently assumed that because I am a deep black democrat I would relish taking part in bringing Professor Mansfield down. To his surprise, and I would imagine embarrassment, I told him that Professor Mansfield is a friend of mine, my former teacher and a respected colleague, and that in fact I had just congratulated Mansfield at the faculty club on his superb translation (with his wife) of Tocqueville's two-volume classic *Democracy in America.* I told Summers that Professor Mansfield and I had taken part in many public debates on race, which had been wildly popular with students, that I had lectured in his classes, and that though I vehemently disagreed with Mansfield's views we never reverted to ugly language or nasty name-calling. President Summers reacted as if I'd transformed from a stereotypical hip-hop ghetto dweller into a Bible-thumping, Sunday-school-attending evangelical believer (which, in part, I am) before his eyes. I was appalled that the president of this country's premier university would take such a bullying and crude approach to his faculty.

With those pleasant formalities over, Summers then launched into a litany of complaints about me and reprimands. He complained that I had canceled classes for three straight weeks in the

year 2000 to promote the Bill Bradley campaign. That I had lent my
support to a presidential candidate no one in his right mind would
support (I wondered whether he meant Ralph Nader or Al
Sharpton, but quickly concluded he meant the latter). He ex-
claimed that my rap CD was an embarrassment to Harvard, and
that I needed to write a major book on a philosophical tradition to
establish myself (he was apparently unaware that I had written just
such a book twelve years earlier, and that I was in fact quite well established, having earlier held tenured positions at both Yale and
Princeton). He then asserted that my course in Afro-American
studies—and other courses in the department—were contributing
to grade inflation in the curriculum. That I had to learn to be a good
citizen at Harvard and focus on the academic needs of students,
not the wages of workers (though, of course, I had just fought to address the needs of students by keeping my most popular class open
to all seven hundred who had enrolled). That I needed to write
works that would be reviewed not in popular periodicals like the
New York Review of Books but in specialized academic journals (no
book of mine has ever been independently reviewed in the *New
York Review of Books*, but there's always hope). And that we should
meet bimonthly so he could monitor my grades and my progress on
published work. He ended his tirade with a sense of reassurance,
which was accompanied by a smug grin of the arrogance I often as-
sociate with the bosses of my late father as they denied him a pro-
motion for the nth time. What kind of reaction could he have
expected from me? What kind of narrow-mindedness would drive
someone in his position of authority to make such irresponsible
characterizations on the basis purely of hearsay and perhaps per-

sonal and political bias? Did he believe he was beyond accountability, like some rash CEO of a corporation?

In response I looked him straight in the eyes and asked him
what kind of person he took me to be. I informed him that I had
missed one class in all my time at Harvard, in order to give the
keynote address at a Harvard-sponsored conference on AIDS in
Addis Ababa, Ethiopia, led by my wife. That I don't support candidates based on what others say or respect, but based on my personal
convictions. That I was as much a part of the Harvard tradition as
he was (I revere the place, having graduated from Harvard College
in 1973) and that if I wanted to present a danceable education to
young people in their own idiom I would do so. That I had written
sixteen books, including a highly respected treatment of the major
American philosophical tradition (pragmatism—from Emerson to
Rorty) still in print after twelve years. That the grades in my courses
could stand next to any grades in any other department. That the
New York Review of Books had never reviewed my books in a major
way. That I had given over fifty lectures to student groups in my
seven years at Harvard. That my office hours were often extended
to five hours to accommodate students. And that I would not mind
meeting him over the year but never to be monitored as if I were his
negligent graduate student. At that our meeting was over.

Though the encounter should never have become news, because
of the explosive nature of the situation—a clash between a prominent black Harvard professor and the brash new Jewish Harvard
president—it became a news bombshell. This experience gave me
a personal taste of the media's crass, sentimental nihilist quest for
the juicy story. After meeting with my close colleagues at Harvard,

I had decided not to go public and simply to resign from Harvard and return to Princeton, an offer that had been extended to me long before, first by Princeton president Harold Shapiro and then by the new president, Shirley Tilghman. But then the rumors began to swirl and news reporters started to appear at my door, and though I refused to say a word, the press had a field day.

The *Boston Globe* ran a piece on the incident by a reporter who had tried to reach me for two months. The *New York Times* followed with a front-page article—without talking to me—that focused on Summers's ambivalence about affirmative action, an issue not even broached in our meeting. The next thing I knew, reporters from around the country and the world were descending on Cambridge to get the scoop on what was *really* happening at Harvard. Students responded with petitions of support. TV pundits were charging me with never showing up for classes, spending all my time in the recording studio, refusing to write books, publishing mediocre texts years ago, and mau-mauing Summers to enhance my salary. George Will even wrote that my position at Harvard was an extreme case of "racial entitlement." In the face of an onslaught like that, and after consulting my friend Professor Charles Ogletree Jr. of Harvard Law School, I decided I had to speak, and did so first with Tavis Smiley and later the *New York Times* and on *The O'Reilly Factor.* My purpose was to tell the truth, expose the lies, and bear witness to the fact that President Summers had messed with the wrong Negro.

Despite the press's focus on me and my alleged transgressions, the image of Harvard was tarnished. The media frenzy had made

Summers look not in control of the situation. When some colleagues threatened to leave with me, the Harvard overseers—his bosses—began to get nervous. The word also spread that I had more academic references in professional journals than all other black scholars in the country except my colleague Professor William Julius Wilson (also a University Professor); that I had more academic references than fourteen of the other seventeen Harvard University Professors; and that I had nearly twice as many such references as Summers himself. It had become clear that he had not done his homework—not read one page of my corpus, not listened to one note of my CD, nor consulted colleagues about my grades or my work with students on campus. Despite the premature wave of support for him in the press, the truth was emerging. So Summers requested another meeting to clear the air, and I accepted.

In our next meeting, Summers was cordial, at ease, and clearly eager to get the matter behind him. We talked movingly about my upcoming surgery (I had cancer at the time) and his courageous experience as a cancer survivor himself. He thanked me for not playing the race card. His major fear in the incident was clearly that he would be pegged as a racist—a charge already leveled at him during his years at the World Bank. I replied that in America the whole deck was full of race cards; I just felt that other issues were also at stake. He said we'd had a mere misunderstanding and apologized—more than once—to me. I replied that he had authorized every xenophobic and conservative or neoliberal newspaper writer in the country to unleash pent-up hostility toward me. And still the media distortions continued.

The next day, a story on the front page of the *New York Times* reported that Summers had not budged an inch, had held his ground against me, and had refused to apologize. I could not believe what I had read and immediately called him and asked him whether he had not in fact apologized—more than once. He said of course he had and that the story had simply gotten it wrong. Unbelievably, I was later to find out that when a contact of mine asked the reporter about the story, and whether Summers had apologized to me, the reporter said that in an interview Summers had strongly insisted that he had not apologized and would never do so. I then knew just what an unprincipled power player I was dealing with. In my next interview I called Summers the Ariel Sharon of American higher education—a bull in a china shop, a bully in a difficult and delicate situation, an arrogant man, and an ineffective leader. Needless to say, more hell broke loose. Charges of anti-Semitism were heard from New York to Tel Aviv—charges I had encountered before, given my support of the Million Man March led by Minister Louis Farrakhan, as well as my staunch opposition with my friend Rabbi Michael Lerner to Sharon's repressive policies against the Palestinians.

The whole ugly incident reflects the crass level to which the university world has sunk; it has become a competitive, market-driven, backbiting microcosm of the troubles with American business and society at large.

My disappointments were threefold. First, how little interest the Harvard faculty and the press had in waiting to ascertain the truth—*veritas*, the very motto of Harvard—as opposed to relishing the swarm of rumor and misstatements. University professors are all too aware of what a backbiting world academic life has become, and yet they showed so little concern about academic freedom and respect for a fellow colleague. This attitude is so representative of a spinelessness in the academy that is antithetical to the important role universities should be playing in holding up standards of truth and integrity and working to impart faith in those standards to our youth.

Second, I was amazed at how parochial and personal the issue was perceived to be. It was viewed as a mere local clash of personalities, with the president upholding standards and refusing to give in to an undeserving and greedy professor. What was missed was the larger issue—a debate about the vision of the national university in the age of American empire. A well-established professor—already tenured at Yale, Princeton, and Harvard, with more publications than 95 percent of his colleagues—was told to tame his fire, limit his audience, and do what he was told in the academy by a Harvard president with a technocratic vision and bullying behavior. Universities are meant to be sanctum sanctorums of robust debate, not institutions run by dictatorial mandate. President Summers has every right to his views about affirmative action, Iraq, hip-hop culture, the Israeli-Palestinian conflict, and a living wage for workers at Harvard. And so do I, and I should have had the right to oppose him and insist on reasonable debate without being subjected to slightly veiled threats and overt disrespect. None of these issues about the integrity of academic freedom surfaced in the worldwide frenzy over the incident. Only a subtle article by Sam Tanenhaus in *Vanity Fair* (June 2002) raised these issues.

Third, the delicate dilemma of black-Jewish relations was boiling beneath the surface of our controversy, yet only Rabbi Michael Lerner had the courage to address it. The first Jewish president of Harvard—an institution with its own history of anti-Semitism and racism—not only comes down on a high-profile African American professor but also challenges the merits of the premier Afro-American Studies Department in the world. The tensions between blacks and Jews are so volatile and our national discourse regarding difficult issues is so stunted that thoughtful dialogue is nearly impossible. Now there is little sensitivity to and awareness of the legacy of that tension at the country's leading university.

The larger message of my sad encounter with President Summers is that it reflects a fundamental clash between the technocratic and the democratic conceptions of intellectual life in America. Summers revealed that he has a great unease about academics engaging the larger culture and society—especially the youths of hip-hop culture and democratic movements of dissent and resistance. My vision of academic engagement embraces his academic standards of excellence yet also revels in overcoming the huge distance between the elite world of the universities, the young people in the hood, and the democratic activists who fight for social change. As one who is deeply committed to the deep democratic tradition in America and to engaging youth culture, I have no intention of cutting back on my academic and outreach activities, because the effort to shatter the sleepwalking of youths who are shut out of the intellectual excitement and opportunity of the academy is such a vital one for our democracy.

It is imperative that young people—of all classes and colors—see that the older generation in the academy cares about them, that we take them seriously, and that we want to hear what they have to say. We must be relentless in our efforts to connect with youth culture in order to impart hard-won wisdom about life's difficult journey— and keep our fragile democratic experiment alive in the future.

7

PUTTING ON
OUR DEMOCRATIC ARMOR

I shall never stop practicing philosophy and exhorting you and elucidating the truth for everyone that I meet. I shall go on saying . . . Are you not ashamed that you give your attention to acquiring as much money as possible, and similarly with reputation and honor and give no attention to truth and understanding and the perfection of your soul? . . . I shall do this to everyone I meet, young or old, foreigner or fellow citizen, but especially to you, my fellow citizens.

—Socrates, from Plato's *Apology* 29d–30a

And Jesus returned in the power of the Spirit into Galilee: and there went out a fame of him through all the region round about. And he taught in their synagogues, being glorified of all. And he came to Nazareth, where he had been brought up: and, as his custom was, he went into the synagogue on the Sabbath day, and stood up to read. And there was delivered unto him the book of the prophet Isaiah. And when he had opened the book, he found the place where it was written,

The Spirit of the Lord is upon me, because he hath anointed me to preach the gospel to the poor; he hath sent me to heal the brokenhearted, to preach deliverance to the captives, and recovering of sight to the blind, to set at liberty them that are oppressed.

—Luke 4:14–18

Democracy is, or should be, the most disinterested form of love.

—RALPH ELLISON, "Letter to Albert Murray," August 17, 1957

In all of Lester Young's finest solos (as in Ellington's always ambivalent foxtrots) there are overtones of unsentimental sad-ness that suggest that he was never unmindful of human vul-nerability and was doing what he was doing with such imperturbable casualness not only in spite of but also as a re-sult of all the trouble he had seen, been beset by, and somehow survived. In a sense, the elegance of earned self-togetherness and with-it-ness so immediately evident in all his quirky lyri-cism is the musical equivalent of the somewhat painful but nonetheless charismatic parade-ground strut of the campaign-weary soldier who has been there one more time and made it back in spite of hell and high water with shrapnel exploding all around him.

—ALBERT MURRAY, *Stomping the Blues* (1976)

September 11 was a deeply traumatic event for us. It shat-tered our illusions of security and invincibility and shocked us about the degree of hatred the terrorists harbored for us. After a brief moment of national unity, disillusionment and division set in. Deep polarization resurfaced with more vengeance as we turned on one another with anger and frustration. The raw debates about Iraq, the Patriot Act, tax cuts, gay marriage, and the down-

and-dirty presidential election of 2004 have left us feeling almost like two countries, disenchanted and, at times, in downright despair. The pervasive depression and disaffection of youth, the flight of so many adults into mindless escapism to combat loneliness and the lack of a sense of purpose in their lives, and the plunge into frenetic consumerism to offset our restlessness all reveal the fissures in our civic life. Neither a new president (though badly needed) nor a fresh administration will satisfy our democratic longings. The profound dismay with our democracy goes beyond the bounds of the current moment.

In our disillusionment with our politicians and plutocrats—and with our media watchdogs—we have focused on the corruptions of our democratic system and have lost our sense of connection to the vital roles played in any democracy by an enlightened and motivated democratic citizenry, and by the principled coalitions that can so effectively push for democratic change. Democracy is not simply a matter of an electoral system in which citizens get the right to vote and elected officials must compete for the public's favor (or find ways to manipulate the public into favoring them, or rig the electoral system to limit competition, as is too often the case today in America). All systems set up to enact democracy are subject to corrupt manipulations, and that is why the public commitment to democratic involvement is so vital. Genuine, robust democracy must be brought to life through democratic individuality, democratic community, and democratic society.

In America, we have tended to underplay the crucial role of the foundational motivation of democracy. From the time of that first Athenian democratic experiment in the fifth century BC to the birth of the American democratic experiment in the eighteenth century, the consolidation of elite power was the primary object of democratic revolt. This will to transform corrupted forms of elite rule into more democratic ways of life is an extraordinary force, though each new democratic result of the exercise of this will falls short of democratic ideals. This is why all democracies are incomplete and unfinished, and this is why American democracy is a work in progress.

We have seen that there are two opposing tendencies in American democracy—toward imperialism and toward democratization—and we are in a period of intense battle between the two. At this moment our imperialist elites are casting themselves as the defenders of our democracy. The Bush administration has subverted the public will in order to lead its war against terrorism in the way it wanted to—attacking Iraq and instituting the dangerous doctrine of preemptive strike rather than focusing on the real terrorist threat. Our business elites have cloaked themselves in the rhetoric of the unfettered free market and of the inevitable juggernaut of corporate globalization, justifying an obscene exacerbation of wealth inequality. It is in the face of such egregious misrepresentations of democracy that the example of the original Greek experiment with democracy—especially the witness of Socrates—is so relevant.

The historic emergence of Athenian democracy and the Greek invention of Socratic dialogue must instruct and inspire our practice of democratic citizenship in present-day America. Athenian democracy was created by the revolt of organized peasants against the abusive power of oligarchic rulers. These peasants refused to be passive victims in the face of plutocratic policies that redistributed wealth upward—from the vast majority to the privileged few. The Greek conception of democracy elevated abused peasants into active citizens who demanded public accountability of their elected officials. Their democratic calls for land reform and the cancellation of debts to greedy elites produced an unprecedented experiment in self-government.

The move away from the rule of kings evolved gradually in Athens, with a crucial step being the separation of authority between the king and the new office of Archon, which assumed many of the operational responsibilities of the government. That reform may have been enacted as early as 1088 BC. In 594 BC, Solon was elected Archon and he responded to the power of organized independent farmers and wealthy nonnoble peasants by establishing legal reforms that incorporated these excluded Athenians into the highest government body (the council of the Areopagus) and into the juries of new courts. These reforms set in motion ideals of equality—of political and judicial equality—and notions of public life predicated on trust between conflicting classes and groups in Athenian society. As Demosthenes, the greatest public orator of his day, proclaimed regarding this democratizing motivation:

> He who claims your indulgence as having acted for
> the good of the commonwealth must be shown to pos-
> sess the spirit of the commonwealth. That spirit is a
> spirit of compassion for the helpless, and of resist-

ance to the intimidation of the strong and powerful;
it does not inspire brutal treatment of the populace,
and subservience to the potentates of the day.

Solon's reforms did not establish Athenian democracy, but they
did constitute a compromise between clashing classes and groups
that put Athens on the road toward democracy. When Cleisthenes
triumphed over his foe Isagoras by siding with the demos in 508
BC, he immediately set in place a new political system of demes.
The demes were vibrant forms of local democratic participation
and communal activity that bring to mind New England township
democracy centuries ago, and they replaced the old Greek system
of kinship tribes based on birth. Like juries, the demes were grassroots training grounds for democratic temperaments that undercut blind allegiances to family, clan, or tribe. In addition,
Cleisthenes established a new democratic council of five hundred
representatives that replaced the old aristocratic council of the
Areopagus. Athenian democracy was born.

This historic evolution from a society and government based
on loyalty to a narrow kinship group into a broader citizenship
model was, in the wonderful phrase of Eli Sagan in his superb book
The Honey and the Hemlock (1991), "the conscious moralization of
democratic energy." And when Pericles ascended to power in 443
BC and later instituted the first pay for public service—along with
a system of annual rotation in office and the lot for holding office—
Athenian democracy was solidified. This experiment was less a
static constitutional order than a dynamic democratic culture of
civic participation. As Sheldon Wolin notes, this "great achieve-

ment of self-government was to transform politics in sight and speech; power was made visible; decision making was opened so that citizens could see its workings; ordinary men personified power, spoke to it unservilely, and held themselves answerable."

This remarkable unleashing of deep democratic energies went hand in hand with clever oligarchic efforts to subvert the will of the demos, whether by overt corruption or covert manipulation. This corruption or manipulation often resulted from the widespread market activity that was widely viewed to be incompatible or at odds with Athenian public life. The Athenians were well aware that the voices of the demos could be offset by powerful market elites bending the system to serve the interests of the few. The economic power of the oligarchs was recognized to be the primary source of the corruptions of Athenian democratic governance.

It is no accident that the Greek invention of Socratic dialogue was motivated, in part, by opposition to the market-driven Sophists obsessed with moneymaking. The major foes of Socrates in the writings that popularized his ideas—like Thrasymachus in Plato's *Republic*—were cast as greedy merchants and clever rhetoricians with little regard for the quality of democratic public life. In fact, the Socratic love of wisdom was contrasted sharply against the Sophistic love of money.

The leading Sophist of the day—Gorgias—was described by Isocrates in the *Antidosis:*

> This man spent time among the Thessalians when
> these people were the wealthiest of the Greeks; he
> lived a long life and was devoted to making money;

he had no fixed dwelling in any city and therefore did
not spend money for the benefit of the public.

And the contemporary historian K. J. Dover writes in his essay "The
Freedom of the Intellectual in Greek Society," the Sophists as intellectuals "were widely regarded as exercising, through their
wealthy Athenian patrons, great influence over Athenian policy,
while not themselves accountable for the execution of policy."

In the great story of Athenian democracy, Socrates is the towering figure precisely because it was his central mission to combat
the corruptions of elite power by questioning the narrow ideological and prejudicial thinking of his day. He was an exemplary democratic citizen—serving on the council and partaking in three major
military campaigns (Potidaea, Delium, and Amphipolis)—and he
took it as his calling to go out to the demos to "infect them also with
the perplexity I feel myself" (Plato, *Meno* 80c–d).

The Socratic love of wisdom holds not only that the unexamined life is not worth living (*Apology* 38a) but also that to be human
and a democratic citizen requires that one muster the courage to
think critically for oneself. This love of wisdom is a perennial pursuit into the dark corners of one's own soul, the night alleys of
one's society, and the back roads of the world in order to grasp
the deep truths about one's soul, society, and world. This pursuit
shatters one's petty idols, false illusions, and seductive fetishes;
it undermines blind conformity, glib complacency, and pathetic
cowardice. Socratic questioning yields intellectual integrity,
philosophic humility, and personal sincerity—all essential ele-

ments of our democratic armor for the fight against corrupt elite power.

Socratic questioning is the enactment of *parrhesia*—frank and fearless speech—that is the lifeblood of any democracy. Socrates admits that *parrhesia* was "the cause of my unpopularity" (*Apology* 24a). And it was the reason for his tragic death. Yet he chose to die rather than live a lie. His noble death—at the hands of dogmatic and nihilistic elites—gave rise to a new literary genre that kept his memory alive. This famous genre of questioning—immortalized by his student Plato—consists of intense interrogation and sustained examination of how we ought to live. It wrestles with basic questions such as, What is justice? What is courage? What is piety? What is love? And although Socrates never wrote a word, Socratic writers like Plato, Xenophon, and Aeschines left powerful and poignant portraits of the democratic practice of Socratic questioning. In fact, Plato's dramatic portraits of this democratic practice constitute the foundations of Western philosophy (*philosophia*, or love of wisdom). The democratic energies of Socratic questioning tend to brazenly and forcefully challenge the corrupt rule of elites and often subject its practitioners to ridicule and censure of various kinds. Yet Socratic questioning is indispensable to any democratic experiment.

Ironically, Plato's love of Socrates and his hatred of those who put Socrates to death—corrupt elites of Athenian democracy—produced a schizophrenia in Plato's thought. As S. Sara Monoson's excellent book, *Plato's Democratic Entanglements* (2000), shows, this schizophrenia is central to Plato's philosophy. On the one hand, his texts embody a vibrant democratic energy of Socratic questioning that shuns the dogmatism and nihilism of corrupt rulers. On the other hand, his vision of order and hierarchy legitimate an antidemocratic authoritarianism. Plato's famous vertical chain of being trumps any democracy. Yet his magnificent development of the Socratic literary genre was rooted in a ferocious scrutiny of the lived experience of the demos. Plato's writings were indebted to poetic forms that focused on the experiences of ordinary Athenians. These forms consisted of the mimes of Sophron and his son Xenarchus and the comedies of Aristophanes. Mimes were a form of popular entertainment, akin to a play, in which actors depicted scenes from everyday life that were focused on revealing aspects of people's character. Both these mimes and the comedies highlighted the lives of lower-class men and women, or "low characters," who were "laughable and without any grandeur." Plato's fear of the blind passions and anarchic potential of the demos led him to use his essentially democratic genre for antidemocratic ends.

His fierce Socratic questioning led to aristocratic conclusions. In Plato's mind, as in the minds of the American Founding Fathers, democratic energies were both appreciated and feared—the voices of the demos required not only acknowledgment but also containment. In book eight of the *Republic*, Plato defines democracy as "a polis full of freedom and frank speech (*Parrhesia*)" that can never resolve the perennial problem of corruption or creeping despotism. For him, only the rule of philosopher-kings equipped with knowledge of the good life could control the unruly passions of the demos. American democracy emerged as a republic (representative government) rather than an Athenian-like direct democracy primarily owing to the same elite fear of the passions and ignorance of the demos. As James Madison notes in his famous sentence in *The Federalist Papers:*

> Had every Athenian citizen been a Socrates every Athenian assembly would still have been a mob.

For the Founding Fathers—just as for Plato—too much Socratic questioning from the demos and too much power sharing of elites with the demos were expected to lead to anarchy, instability, or perpetual rebellion. The democratic genius of the Founding Fathers was to nevertheless incorporate Socratic questioning into our government in the form of a procedure for constitutional revision and to create the Bill of Rights to protect *parrhesia*, despite their fear of the unruly demos. Without these Socratic dimensions of American democracy, American tyranny would have triumphed. Without Socratic questioning by the demos, elite greed at home and imperial domination abroad devour any democracy.

As the great Reinhold Niebuhr noted, democracy is a proximate solution to insoluble problems—it is always messy and subject to corrupt manipulation, yet it is still the best civic project for the demos. Does not Thucydides' classic *History of the Peloponnesian War* lay bare the insidious seeds of domestic greed and imperial domination as the primary causes of the decay and decline of Athenian democracy? The Macedonian and Roman dominations of a weak and corrupt Athenian democracy were the ugly results of these poisonous seeds. Can we learn from this tragic example? Only if we avoid the paralyzing paranoia of Manichaean thinking, the debilitating hubris of dogmatic arrogance, and the myopic self-righteousness of nihilistic imperialism. And we avoid these best when we are Socratic as individuals, as communities, and as a society. The fragile health of a democracy rests upon the Socratic health of its demos. As the wise and reluctant democrat Matthew Arnold, an English critic and poet, concluded in his classic *Culture and Anarchy* (1869):

> . . . but in his own breast does not every man carry about with him a possible Socrates, in that power of a disinterested play of consciousness upon his stock notions and habits, of which this wise and admirable man gave all through his lifetime the great example, and which was the secret of his incomparable influence? And he who leads men to call forth and exercise in themselves this power, and who busily calls it forth and exercises it in himself, is at the present moment, perhaps, as Socrates was in his time, more in concert with the vital working of men's minds, and more effectually significant, than any . . . practical operator in politics.

This Arnoldian sentiment is expressed in an American idiom by Ralph Waldo Emerson, the godfather of our deep democratic tradition, in his essay "Plato; or the Philosopher," a tribute to the Socrates of Plato's texts:

The rare coincidence, in one ugly body, of the droll
and the martyr, the keen street and market debater
with the sweetest saint known to any history at that
time, had forcibly struck the mind of Plato, so capa-
cious of these contrasts; and the figure of Socrates,
by a necessity, placed itself in the foreground of the
scene, as the fittest dispenser of the intellectual treas-
ures he had to communicate. It was a rare fortune,
that this Aesop of the mob, and this robed scholar,
should meet, to make each other immortal in their
mutual faculty.

For Emerson, every democratic citizen must aspire to the
Socratic love of wisdom, to a vigilant questioning that transforms
the unruly mob into mature seekers of the tougher, deeper truths
that sustain democratic individuals, democratic communities, and
democratic societies.

Yet our Socratic questioning must go beyond Socrates. We must
out-Socratize Socrates by revealing the limits of the great Socratic
tradition. My own philosophy of democracy that emerges from the
nightside of American democracy is rooted in the guttural cries
and silent tears of oppressed people. And it has always bothered me
that Socrates never cries—he never sheds a tear. His profound yet
insufficient rationalism refuses to connect noble self-mastery to a
heartfelt solidarity with the agony and anguish of oppressed peoples. Why this glaring defect in Socratic love of wisdom? Does not
the rich Socratic legacy of Athens need the deep prophetic legacy

of Jerusalem? Must not the rigorous questioning and quest for wisdom of the Socratic be infused with the passionate fervor and quest for justice of the prophetic?

The Jewish invention of the prophetic begins with the cries for help and tears of sorrow of an oppressed people. This profound grief and particular grievances are directed against imperial Egypt. God hears their cries and is moved by their tears because God is first and foremost a lover of justice (Psalms 99:4 and 37:28; Isaiah 61:8). The Judaic God declares, "I will surely hear their cry. . . . For I am compassionate" (Exodus 22:23, 27). Divine compassion undergirds the divine love of justice just as human compassion undergirds the prophetic love of justice. The premier prophetic language is the language of cries and tears because human hurt and misery give rise to visions of justice and deeds of compassion. For the prophetic tradition, the cries and tears of an oppressed people signify an alternative to oppression and symbolize an allegiance to a God who requires human deeds that address these cries and tears.

The Christian movement that emerged out of prophetic Judaism made the language of cries and tears a new way of life and struggle in the world. My philosophy of democracy is deeply shaped by that particular Jew named Jesus who put the love of God and neighbor at the core of his vision of justice and his deeds of compassion. His vision of a just future consoles those who cry and his deeds of compassion comfort those who shed tears. His loving gift of ministry, grace, and death under the rule of nihilistic imperial elites enacts divine compassion and justice in human flesh. The ultimate Christian paradox of God crucified in history under the Roman empire is that the love and justice that appear so weak may be strong, that seem so foolish may be wise, and that strike imperial elites as easily disposable may be inescapably indispensable. The prophetic tradition is fueled by a righteous indignation at injustice—a moral urgency to address the cries and tears of oppressed peoples.

Despite the Constantinian captivity of much of the Christian movement here and abroad, the prophetic tradition has a deep legacy of providing extraordinary strength of commitment and vision that helps us to care in a palpable way about the injustices we see around us. In our own time this was the fire that drove Martin Luther King Jr., Rabbi Abraham Joshua Heschel, Dorothy Day, and millions of other Americans to deepen our democratic project. This prophetic tradition is an infectious and invigorating way of life and struggle. It generates the courage to care and act in light of a universal moral vision that indicts the pervasive corruption, greed, and bigotry in our souls and society. It awakens us from the fashionable ways of being indifferent to other people's suffering or from subtle ways of remaining numb to the social misery in our midst. Prophetic love of justice unleashes ethical energy and political engagement that explodes all forms of our egocentric predicaments or tribalistic mind-sets. Its telling signs are ethical witness (including maybe martyrdom for some), moral consistency, and political activism—all crucial elements of our democratic armor for the fight against corrupt elite power.

Yet in our postmodern world of pervasive consumerism and hedonism, narcissism and cynicism, skepticism and nihilism, the Socratic love of wisdom and prophetic love of justice may appear hopeless. Who has not felt overwhelmed by dread and despair when confronting the atrocities and barbarities of our world? And surely a cheap optimism or trite sentimentalism will not sustain us. We need a bloodstained Socratic love and tear-soaked prophetic love fueled by a hard-won tragicomic hope. Our democratic fight against corrupt elite power needs the vital strength provided by the black American invention of the blues. The blues is the most profound interpretation of tragicomic hope in America. The blues encourages us to confront the harsh realities of our personal and political lives unflinchingly without innocent sentimentalism or coldhearted cynicism. The blues forges a mature hope that fortifies us on the slippery tightrope of Socratic questioning and prophetic witness in imperial America.

This black American interpretation of tragicomic hope is rooted in a love of freedom. It proceeds from a free inquisitive spirit that highlights imperial America's weak will to racial justice. It is a sad yet sweet indictment of abusive power and blind greed run amok. It is a melancholic yet melioristic stance toward America's denial of its terrors and horrors heaped on others. It yields a courage to hope for betterment against the odds without a sense of revenge or resentment. It revels in a dark joy of freely thinking, acting, and loving under severe constraints of unfreedom.

I have always marveled at how such an unfree people as blacks in America created the freest forms in America, such as blues and jazz. I have often pondered how we victims of American democracy invented such odes to democratic individuality and community as in the blues and jazz. And I now wonder whether American democracy can survive without learning from the often-untapped democratic energies and lessons of black Americans. How does one affirm a life of mature autonomy while recognizing that evil is inseparable from freedom? How does one remain open and ready for meaningful solidarity with the very people who hate you? Frederick Douglass and Bessie Smith, Ida B. Wells-Barnett and Duke Ellington, Sarah Vaughan and Martin Luther King Jr., Ella Baker and Louis Armstrong all are wise voices in a deep democratic tradition in America that may provide some clue to these crucial questions in our time. They all knew that even if the tears of the world are a constant quantity and that the air is full of our cries, we can and should still embark on a democratic quest for wisdom, justice, and freedom.

This kind of tragicomic hope is dangerous—and potentially subversive—because it can never be extinguished. Like laughter, dance, and music, it is a form of elemental freedom that cannot be eliminated or snuffed out by any elite power. Instead, it is inexorably resilient and inescapably seductive—even contagious. It is wedded to a long and rich tradition of humanist pursuits of wisdom, justice, and freedom from Amos through Socrates to Ellison. The high modern moments in this tradition—Shakespeare, Beethoven, Chekhov, Coltrane—enact and embody a creative weaving of the Socratic, prophetic, and tragicomic elements into profound interpretations of what it means to be human. These three elements constitute the most sturdy democratic armor available to us in our fight against corrupt elite power. They represent the best of what has been bequeathed to us and what we look like when we are at our best—as deep democrats and as human beings.

This democratic armor allows us to absorb any imperial and xenophobic blows yet still persist. It permits us to face any antidemocratic foe and still persevere. It encourages us to fight any form of dogma or nihilism and still endure. It only requires that we be true to ourselves by choosing to be certain kinds of human beings and democratic citizens indebted to a deep democratic tradition and committed to keeping it vital and vibrant. This democratic vocation wedded to an unstoppable predilection for possibility may not guarantee victory, but it does enhance the probability of hard-won progress. And if we lose our precious democratic experiment, let it be said that we went down swinging like Ella Fitzgerald and Muhammad Ali—with style, grace, and a smile that signifies that the seeds of democracy matters will flower and flourish somewhere and somehow and remember our gallant efforts.

ACKNOWLEDGMENTS

This book was made possible—as are all of my writings—by my loving family: my inimitable parents, the late Clifton L. West and Irene Bias West (the precious namesake of the recently dedicated Irene B. West Elementary School!); my steadfast brother, Clifton L. West (the deepest person I know); my supportive sisters, Cynthia McDaniel and Cheryl West; my wonderful son, Clifton Louis West; and my lovely daughter, Dilan Zeytun West. I benefited greatly from the professional support of Mary Ann Rodriguez and the personal love of Leslie Oser Kotkin. The hard work of Ben Polk and the editorial genius of Emily Loose made this work much of what it is. I also want to thank my blessed literary agent, Gloria Loomis, and the visionary publisher Ann Godoff. I take full responsibility for its shortcomings.

PERMISSIONS

INDEX

ABOUT THE AUTHOR

Cornel West is Class of 1943 University Professor of Religion at Princeton University. He has held positions at Union Theological Seminary, Yale University, Harvard University, and the University of Paris. He has written numerous books, including *Race Matters, The American Evasion of Philosophy,* and *The Cornel West Reader.* His *Beyond Eurocentrism and Multiculturalism* (vols. 1 and 2) won the American Book Award.